THE STERLING BOOK OF
MA SARADA

Titles in the Series

1. The Sterling Book of **Indian Classical Dances**
   – *Shovana Narayan*

2. The Sterling Book of **Buddha and His Teaching**
   – *Kingsley Heendeniya*

3. The Sterling Book of **Ma Sarada: The Miracle of Love**
   – *Prof M Sivaramkrishna*

4. The Sterling Book of **Bhagwad Gita**
   – *O P Ghai*

5. The Sterling Book of **Hinduism**
   – *Karan Singh*

THE STERLING BOOK OF
MA SARADA
The Miracle of Love

Prof M Sivaramkrishna

NEW DAWN PRESS, INC.
UK • USA • INDIA

*Dedicated
to
Sri Ram*

NEW DAWN PRESS GROUP

Published by New Dawn Press Group

New Dawn Press, 2 Tintern Close, Slough, Berkshire, SL1-2TB, UK
e-mail: ndpuk@newdawnpress.com

New Dawn Press, Inc., 244 South Randall Rd # 90, Elgin, IL 60123, USA
e-mail: sales@newdawnpress.com

New Dawn Press (An Imprint of Sterling Publishers (P) Ltd.)
A-59, Okhla Industrial Area, Phase-II, New Delhi-110020, INDIA
e-mail: info@sterlingpublishers.com
www.sterlingpublishers.com

The Sterling Book of: Ma Sarada
Copyright © 2005 by M Sivaramkrishna
ISBN 1 84557 203 3

All rights are reserved. No part of this publication may be reproduced, stored in a retrieval system or transmitted, in any form or by any means, mechanical, photocopying, recording or otherwise, without prior written permission of the original publisher.

Preface

This volume contains glimpses of the unique life of Sri Sarada Devi, the divine consort of Sri Ramakrishna Paramahamsa. It combines both her human and divine roles. It was my good fortune to be initiated during the birth centenary of the Mother (1953) by Revered Swami Yatiswaranandaji, the then Vice-President of the Ramakrishna order. This book is the result of his blessings.

The core inspiration of the book comes from the benignly anonymous presence of 'Sri Ram' for which no words of gratitude can be adequate. My heartfelt gratitude to him is also due to his gracious acceptance of the dedication.

To Mr Badari Venkata Reddy, Advocate, High Court, Andhra Pradesh, a word of special and deep gratitude for supporting the publication. To Kalikrishna, my son, and his family at New Delhi, thanks are due for providing the right ambience where this book could be written. I am grateful to Sastry and Madhavi for computerizing the book. To Sumita and Chandrima Roy for all their help. I am grateful to the publishers whose sources I have used to draw the incidents of the book.

Finally I must thank Mr S K Ghai and all the members of Sterling Publishers for their immense help and dedicated service in bringing out the book in record time.

M. Sivaramkrishna

3 January 2005

Birth Anniversary of Sarada Devi

Contents

	Preface	5
	Introduction	9
1.	I Am Myself Mahamaya!	11
2.	Ma Kneads Bread	14
3.	My True Self Came Out	19
4.	You Wanted One I Will Give You Two!	23
5.	They Too Are My Children	26
6.	He Would Have Drowned Himself in the Ganga	30
7.	Here Puja Is Done Only for Her	34
8.	Dashing Down Like an Arrow	36
9.	She Heard a Jingling Sound	40
10.	Does She Not Know Who You Are?	43
11.	I Cannot Forget the Child	47
12.	Mere Play of Mahamaya	51

13.	White for the Master, Yellow for Me	56
14.	Why Not?	59
15.	When You Say She Will be Cured, She *Shall* be Cured	62
16.	It Has Become Mischievous	67
17.	Beings All Over the Universe Are My Children	69
18.	Let Me Not Grow	73
19.	You Are But My Children	78
20.	How Innocent Is Our Mother	82
21.	*Pipeelikadi Brahma Paryantam!*	85
22.	Call on the Mother Alone!	90
23.	A Porter But a Chosen One!	94
24.	Called Compassionate: But No Trace of It!	97
25.	No Use Repairing It. It Reminds Me of Yogin!	100
26.	If You Want Peace . . .	106
27.	Not Just *Darshan* But Initiation Too	108
28.	No Complaints, Please!	110
29.	The Divine Mother Who Fans and Feeds	113
30.	Fault Finders All: But Let Me Be An Exception!	117
31.	Touch *Me*, That's Enough	120
32.	Forgive Her, She Doesn't Know What She Is Doing	123
33.	Nothing Is Valueless: Everything Is Vibrant	126

Introduction

Sri Sarada Devi, known to devotees also as the Holy Mother or Sri Sri Ma, was born in Jayarambati of West Bengal on 22nd December 1853. She was the eldest child of her parents, Ramachandra Mukherjee and Shyamasundari Devi. At the age of five she was married to Gadadhar of Kamarpukur, later known as the sage of Dakshineswar, Sri Ramakrishna. The Holy Mother was an ideal daughter, an ideal wife and later an ideal Mother to the millions of 'children' who flocked round her.

The Master and the Mother had an ideal relationship. He worshipped her as Shodashi, the Divine Mother of the Universe and laid the fruits of his austerities at her feet. The Mother was in her teens at this time but did not hesitate to accept this highest honour since she knew that her Master found no difference between his own Mother Kali and Sri Sri Ma. She truly manifested exceptional qualities for the remaining four and a half decades of her life.

The Mother lived with her parents till 1872 and from then on, with intermittent breaks she was with her divine husband in Dakshineswar and later at Cossipore till the Master left his mortal frame in 1886. After this she again lived for some time in Kamarpukur and Jayarambati amid great poverty and hardship, especially at the former place. Later she divided her time equally between these two villages and Calcutta till the end of her stay on earth, that is, 1920.

The Mother's life is a mixture of the mundane and the profoundly spiritual. She effortlessly moved from the grossly external to the supremely internal levels of existence all through her life. She faced tremendous hardships with a serenity that is almost impossible to encounter elsewhere. Each incident of her life serves as a core for contemplating on the highest truths embedded in our ancient scriptures and paradoxically in our own ordinary lives. Hence the immediacy and impact of her life on countless women devotees, both Eastern and Western.

All the incidents in the book are drawn from mainly three sources: *The Gospel of the Holy Mother*, Chennai, Sri Ramakrishna Math, *Sarada Ma, the Great Wonder*, New Delhi, Ramakrishna Mission and *The Compassionate Mother Sarada Devi*, Malaysia. I am grateful to all these publishers. Though I have drawn the main incidents from these sources, the portrayal of these is my own. The persons who appear in the narrative are direct disciples of the Master and the devotees of the Mother.

Writing the book was for me an extended meditation with constant inspiration from the Mother. I hope this book will delight readers and devotees alike.

Chapter One
I Am Myself Mahamaya!

A revelation as rare as it is candid. Mother, moreover, reveals the Reality of her manifestation, so casually and in contexts which are least congruous with her being: that itself is unique.

Contrast the Master and the Mother in this regard. On the eve of his passing from the physical frame, which incredibly held condensed cosmic consciousness, the Master declared to the doubting Naren: "He who was Rama and Krishna then, is the same Ramakrishna now!" And he added, "Not in your *Advaitic* sense!"

And the Mother?

Banaras, the holy city, was the locale. The Great Master himself had visited this city of light, of transparent effulgence. He had seen the great God Maha Shiva himself whispering into the ears of the dead the sacred syllables which saved their souls and secured their liberation. He thus validated the faith that held the devotees for times immemorial.

Now the Holy Mother was in this city. And one can say: if the Incarnate Shiva visited his own immortal abode , can his Shakti lag behind? She has to complete the power behind the Shiva-Shakti *sangama tantra*!

Ma visited many places, many sadhus and, perhaps, almost all the sacred places. Did they, one wonders now, realize the tremendous fact that the one on whom they were meditating and whom they held as the object of their *sadhana,* is standing before them? In flesh and blood? The prospect of guessing (let alone *perceiving*) the fact is remote. For the simple reason that impenetrable anonymity is her characteristic stance! None could go beyond the constricted space of this anonymity – like the space of that equally incredible abode: Nahabat!

On that day Ma was especially busy, there was the problem child Radhi to be handled. And, of course, Bhudev and others in her entourage. Arrangements for their food, for their resting – mats, cots, beds, one can imagine – had to be ensured. Each had his/her own idiosyncrasy in everything.

"Ma! Some women devotees are here to have your *darshan*!" announced a devotee who accompanied Ma to Banaras.

"Now! What a time they have chosen!" exclaimed Ma. "All right. It does not matter. Show them in!" said Ma.

The women trooped in. They were all local devotees. And obviously they all came with high expectations. To see evident insignia of a divine nature, to be expected, they firmly believed, in the consort of the famed Paramahamsa. Ma greeted them but carried on with her chores.

"Bhudev! Did you keep some milk for Radhi?"

Bhudev nodded. And turning to another devotee who was helping her, Ma asked.

I Am Myself Mahamaya!

"What about vegetables? Have you gone to the market? You must be careful. We are not locals. You may be cheated."

"No Ma! I am going now. Yes Ma. I shall be careful!" the devotee replied.

Ma then assigned the job of trimming the lanterns as there was still light. The women visitors watched all this almost aghast. Who is this lady immersed in all these worldly matters and yet who is adored as the peer of the great Ramakrishna? they wondered. They could never imagine her to be immersed in *samsara*. Perhaps, they had come to the wrong place, seeing the wrong person. But they were sure this was the Holy Mother. The only thing was the strange incongruity, between what they saw and what they had imagined. One of the devotees couldn't contain herself; as, perhaps, few could, she took to irony and "blurted out":

"Mother! What a strange thing we see! You who we expect to free us from Maya are yourself immersed in it! Samsara has taken hold of you!"

The Mother smiled and said almost to herself: "Well, what to do, my dear, for I myself am Maya!"

Why did the Mother whisper this fact? The ironical reason is the devotee who saw her *saw* the fact but didn't *see through* it. For, as the poet rightly says: "Human kind cannot bear to see very much reality!"

Ma quickly resumed her enacting: "Golap! Would you mind mending that torn cloth?" she asked.

The women devotees found their surprise reach its zenith. Ma who mends the torn cloth of our lives requesting Golap to do it for her! Indeed, who is there who can understand what Ma Mahamaya is!

Chapter Two
Ma Kneads Bread

Is it for nothing that Ma in her manifestation at Kashi is called "Annapurna"? The Mother who represents the plenitude of food, serves food to everyone! And, therefore, no wonder that Holy Mother, our Ma, never failed to feed any visitor or devotee who crossed her threshold, either at Jayarambati or at Udbodhan. Invariably, she prepared the food herself.

But one strange thing is: the kitchen chronicles conceptualize Ma's teachings and revelations. In these apparently routine jobs, we find casual, indeed hardly noticed, epiphanies. Ma ensnares us with a commonplace context and invariably ensures that our attention is deflected.

Arupananda goes to see the Mother. Three or four o'clock in the afternoon. Most women's resting period, their siesta time. But Ma, ever at work, was kneading dough. One can, I suppose, easily visualize Ma sitting on the floor. With legs stretched on the floor. The legs had bore patiently almost life-long pain, often intolerable.

Ma Kneads Bread — 15

When the Swami approaches, she gives him her disarming smile. We don't have photos which catch Ma's smile. Imagination can easily conjure up that subdued smile. It is easily comparable to her Lord and Master's singularly enchanting smile.

The Swami had very crucial questions to ask. The time is propitious. Mother, he knew, is always gracious, willing to look after every need of her devotees.

"Mother, they all say, and we all believer Thakur is God Incarnate. He is the Eternal Reality who took a human form for conferring the inestimable gift of freedom from fear to humanity. Am I right, Mother?"

"Absolutely. To me He is God Himself. Don't you know for the wife, her husband is God Himself!" Mother replied.

The ringing words were irrevocable, firm.

"But, Ma… ," Arupananda started saying.

"You still have a doubt?" asked Mother.

Arupananda is in a fix. He knew the fact of Thakur being the peer of Sri Ramachandra and Sri Krishna. And, naturally Mother is the incarnate form of Sita and Radha. Then how is it she is burdening herself with all these chores, the jobs which an average woman in any household is saddled with? Is she not deluding us into believing that there is nothing exceptional about her? Could anyone conceive Thakur, like an ordinary householder, going to the Dakshineswar market and bringing brinjals and other vegetables? For Ma to cook!

The Swami thought he *must* get an answer.

"I am not saying that. I know for the wife her husband is God Himself," the Swami told Ma.

"Yes, Master is God in a general sense as well," clarified Mother.

"Then how come the Divine Consort of the great Master kneads dough and prepares bread for her children as any ordinary woman does in any home?" the Swami asked.

"Yes. I do everything that a woman in a household has to…," Ma didn't complete.

"Then *it is Maya*, is it not?" the Swami cut in.

One wonders now at this seemingly simple scene, obviously designed by Ma herself. In her *lila*, the Cosmic Play, the ordinary becomes transfused into the extraordinary. And the extraordinary unobtrusively and naturally slips in. The wonder is no Master Mahashaya is needed to construct any scaffolding! The scene unrolls itself according to her wish, her whim, her *iccha*! That's what makes her the great wonder. The Swami was simply delivering the dialogue, the script written for him by this *Saraswati*!

"It is, indeed, Maya," pat came the answer from Ma. "Or else how would you see me in such a state?" added Ma.

"There *must* be a reason for such acts, am I right, Ma?" the Swami asked.

"Quite right. Don't you know what the Master used to say: When God assumes a human form, he is subject to all that goes to be human. Sri Krishna was born a cowherd boy and Rama as the child of Dasaratha," clarified the Mother.

Ma Kneads Bread

The disciple felt intrigued. So far, it is right. But does Ma ever remember her real – her *Sahaja* natural – *tattva*, that she is the Divine Mother herself?

"Ma! Can I ask you something more? Or, am I annoying you by all this talk!" he asked.

The dough-kneading Ma looked up. Smiled. "Why should any child annoy Mother? Go ahead and ask." Ma said.

"Do you – ever – recall your real nature?"

"Of course, I do. Occasionally. I then begin to wonder, and ask myself: 'What is this I am doing? What is all this about?'"

The Swami was, obviously listening to all this with rapt attention. These, indeed, are rare moments. Of immortal epiphanic power, a startling revelation. Comparable, in essence, to those like the majestic scene that shows Krishna's cosmic form. But how gently, naturally, the revelation comes here. And, for that very reason, how effortlessly, easily we forget the revelatory power behind such scenes. Perhaps, in a later day context, when delusion has become thicker and deeper, it is not in one scene alone that epiphany comes. At several places in many contexts Ma gives us glimpses.

Ma's voice cuts in: "Then I remember the house, buildings and children …. And forget my real self!"

And unless she forgets, can we get near her? Can we even look at that Mystery? Unless, as she herself said: "It's only by acceptation of an illusion that I am so. This is nothing but continuing in the midst of an illusion." Aren't We harrowed with fear and wonder? For, meditate on the clinching, absolutely conclusive unveiling that follows a few days later:

"Are you the Mother of all?" the disciple asks pointblank.

Like a flash of lightning that pierces the dark landscape comes Ma's affirmation, "Yes…"

"Even of these birds and animals?"

"Yes, of them also."

One murmurs to oneself: *"Ya devi sarva bhuteshu matrirupena samsthitha…."* The one who is manifest in all living beings as the Mother! Salutations to her again and again.

I began identifying Ma with Annapurna. Do you think it is my fancy? Then look at this! Mother's niece was keen on going to Kashi and asked Ma for permission. She was adamant. Ma asked "Nalini! Why are you keen on going to Kashi? Will Kashi Annapurna talk to you as I do?"

Chapter Three
My True Self Came Out

Myriad are the manifestations of Ma. The ordinary ones trap us into unawareness. We forget – repeatedly – the grandeur, the splendor behind that seemingly anonymous, disarmingly homely exterior. But then glimpses come: intermittent but unmistakable. And when they come, we seem to perceive the recurrence of the Ancient, Primeval Mother's manifestations. Perhaps, the archetypes of the "Dasa Mahavidyas" offer the clue!

Ma was staying at Kamarpukur. The village blessed by the birth of the blissful Master. The *punyasthala*, which is now a significant landmark on the sacred geography of spiritual world, was a few miles away from Jayarambati, the joyful abode of Ma's advent. Mother used to come to Kamarpukur, as per Master's advice – after his passing away. It was here that the Master, Ma said, "appeared before me and asked me to feed him with *khichuri*. I cooked the dish and offered it before Raghuvir in the temple. Then I mentally fed the Master with it."

Obviously the village was surcharged with the Presence of the Master, both visible and subtle.

Ma was staying there. On this day, she went to a neighbor's place and returned home after the visit. Then happened the apparently bizarre incident. Ma herself narrated it. And it figures a devotee called Harish.

It so coincided that at that very moment when Ma was reaching her place, Harish saw her. By then itself he was in a distracted state. To put it bluntly, out of his mind. As soon as he saw Ma, he chased her!

The situation got compounded because there was no one in the house. Imagine: Mother alone there. No one to control a mentally deranged man. We later learnt that he lost his balance because of his wife. Money and matrimony are the twin traps – *Kamini, Kanchana* as Master put it – that created havoc in the life of Harish. To the extent that he was now chasing Ma herself. A piquant situation, indeed.

Let us hear what Ma herself said: "There was then no one else in the house. I did not know where to go, and ran quickly behind the barn. He would not, however, leave me. I ran and ran round it seven times till I got exhausted."

Then happens the most electrifying – rather, the most terrifying – scene:

"Then my true self came out. I threw him to the ground, pressed my knees on his chest, drew out his tongue and slapped him hard on the cheeks until my fingers became red with slapping. He began to gasp for breath."

What a terrifying context. And one notices the paradox: because of circling the barn seven times, Ma says she got exhausted. Did she? Nothing like it! For, in the very next moment Ma reveals the extraordinary transformation that took place. Her *true self came out*. Oh my Ma! We feel like shouting with fear. For, her true self is the very embodiment of colossal, cosmic energy that not only creates and sustains, but dissolves and destroys, too. She is the Mahishasura Mardini, the Kali that protects but punishes when necessary.

One recalls that unique vision, her Lord and Master had: Master saw a woman heavy with a child in the womb, coming out of (primeval?) waters, in no time giving birth to a child and equally in no time dashing its brains out. What the Master saw in his visionary lenses, Ma enacted!

Otherwise – that is, unless there is "a sea change" – how can an exhausted lady, instead of panting for breath, throw the chaser to the ground, (don't forget the fact that mad fellows are stronger than they naturally are!) drew the tongue, and slapped him – until her fingers become red! Red is the colour of anger and throwing on the ground someone who had to be chained – these are all symbolically appropriate.

We also notice one difference: Ma draws out not *her* tongue but the chaser's! Does it suggest a *prayojana*? A function? One thinks, it does. Just as Ma frames the scene in such a way that no one comes to her help. Indeed, we know that Ma wrote to Belur Math to send somebody since Harish was at large in Kamarpukur. Saradanandaji and Niranjanandaji did arrive but it was "just before their arrival" that Ma's real "true self came out". Mother of all does not need anyone to punish her prodigal son.

But then why pull out Harish's tongue? One explanation we have: 'Commenting on the meaning of the words "my true nature came out", the note in Ma's gospel says:

"....Mother being a manifestation of the Divine Devi, could take any form, that she wanted. In this instance, the consciousness of Bagala, one of the Mahavidyas, must have been on her, as Bagala is said to have killed one Asura, in the same manner as the Mother now punished Harish."

The tongue-pulling could, in these terms, as well be, to reform Harish. For we learn that this punishment had a salutary effect on Harish. He fled to Vrindavan and gradually his mental equilibrium was restored.

One can, perhaps, hazard the guess that pulling out Harish's tongue by Ma is a parallel to Master's removal of obstacles from the mind of a devotee by writing something on his tongue!

To clinch all implications, let us meditate on the extraordinary and rare testimony of Bhanupishi which confirms that what we said so far is not the romantic effusion of an enthusiast. Says Bhanupishi:

"One day I saw Mother with four arms. When she was facing me, I saw her in the ordinary form with two arms but when she was showing her back to me, I saw her with four arms. Another day, I told Mother, 'When you sing, I hear the songs of Thakur.' Mother said, 'What do I know? You know better!' I told Mother, 'Thakur is within you.' Mother replied, 'Do you see four hands in me?'"

We are inclined to say, "Yes, Ma we do!"

For, we realize that You are the incarnate form of the deity of Jayarambati who is none other than Simhavahini!

Chapter Four
You Wanted One, I Will Give You Two!

"Whatever you yearn for, that you will get," affirmed Mother. The significant word is *whatever*. Mother makes no hierarchy: "Ask me for mukti," she doesn't say or "Ask me for initiation." Like that she doesn't stipulate what to ask for; or, rather, she has no distinctions in fulfilling our desires. *Anything you ask, she gives*. No question. Only be careful about what you ask. As that wish-fulfilling tree in Thakur's story, a tiger (of worldliness) may come and devour you.

They were four aspirants for *diksha* from Ma. From Baligunj they were going to Jayarambati. On the way another, Shibu Babu, joined them. Mother was delighted, naturally.

"Come! Children. You have come from quite a distance. Go have a wash. Freshen up. And take a cup of tea," Ma said.

Seeing Ma – her *darshan* – is enough to energise. The bonus is tea. They sat on the ground and tea was served. Ma, perhaps, went inside.

"I want to take an egg, Surendra! Can I ask for it?" asked Shibu Babu.

"No. You take whatever is given. And don't make a fuss!" Surendra silenced him.

Perhaps, we also wonder why Shibu should *ask* for something. On the other hand, should we not? If we are not free with Ma, who else can we be with? Don't all our thoughts, emotions, etc, come from that source? And, we *know* for certain that this is the truth, the whole truth.

Two days later they all sat joyously at lunchtime. It was not known whether they received *diksha* or not. The radiance of the place and of the Mother filled their hearts with a tranquil happiness that they never had experienced. This is what quite often happened. The happiness is communicated through channels we know not, (nor need to know). "A pitcher of joy!" The image used by Mother herself.

They were eating the *prasad* with reverence. Mother was watching with her characteristically affectionate eyes. The devotees were halfway through.

"Ma! How can we – indeed in what way can we express our immense gratitude to you?" said Surendra.

"Does anyone express gratitude to his/her Mother?" asked Ma. Surendra and others remained silent. Breaking the silence Ma called Nalini:

"Nalini! Please bring those eggs we got ready for these boys."

One can imagine easily the surprise on the faces of the devotees. But a greater surprise was in store for them. Mother pointed to Shibu Babu and said:

"Give two eggs to Shibu and one each to the rest. You know why? Poor boy, on that very day they came he wanted an egg. But the other boys stopped him from asking!"

The devotees, one can imagine, were listening to this with shock and surprise. How did Ma know?

"You know what?" continued Ma. "Desires are bound to come. We should not keep our desires unfulfilled. By satisfying them, they will fall off slowly in course of time!"

Shibu dissolved into tears. Contemplating the event, we too, today.

And wonder! At the exquisite artistry with which Ma kept two dimensions of her radiance balanced. The one is her *omniscience*; she is *sarvantaryami*. *Anda, Pinda, brahmanda* in here in her *Hiranya garbha*! Cosmic womb which keeps, nourishes all the three poised in between the macrocosm and microcosm.

The other is the nature of desire. Pompously, we call it the dialectic of desire. How naturally Ma makes fulfillment of desires as the natural process of their falling off. Like, as the Master said, leaves falling off the tree! Neither suppression nor indulgence. But their natural transcendence.

Ma herself never advocated torturing the body by fasting and other fetishes. Indeed, in another context Ma firmly said: "If the Atman wants to eat anything, it should be given. If you do not give, it is wrong and ends in punishment. The Atman weeps – you did not give me food, you deprived me of it!"

Chapter Five
They Too Are My Children

It is a paradox that paradox is the key that unlocks the uniqueness of an *avatara*. For, they act and say different things in different contexts. What they affirm at one point, they annul in another. Context-sensitive sensibility marks their actions and in turn their feelings.

The monks at Koalpara Ashrama were all agog. Mother said that on her way to Calcutta, she would stop at their ashrama and spend some time. "You have built a room for the Master," she said and added, "on my way I shall install the Master there." She wanted them to make all arrangements for that. Perhaps with a twinkle in her eyes, Ma said further: "What will you gain by constantly harping on swadeshi? Our roots are in the Master. Hold fast to them."

Ma touched them by the nerve center of many of the monks staying at Koalpara ashram. They were swayed by strong nationalist sentiments of serving the country and wresting freedom from the British. They were inspired, indeed electrified and energized, by Swamiji's patriotism, his

They Too Are My Children

burning zeal to serve the country. This attitude was so strong that one of the monks told Ma:

"Mother! Swamiji exhorted us to work tirelessly for the nation. Were he alive today, one can well imagine how much he would have done to bring freedom for the country!"

"But, he would also have been locked up in a jail by the British government, don't you think? And do you think I could bear to see my beloved Naren going to a prison?" Ma replied, instantly.

Her eyes, one can well imagine, were filled with tears. She must have recalled his presence in the *lila* enacted at Dakshineswar. Naren's vibrant presence, his soul-stirring singing – which often made her Lord plunge into ecstasy – even his skepticism, his reluctance to take anything on trust without testing and above all his deep, unparalleled love for the Master and herself....

"You know, dear," Mother continued, "Naren is an unsheathed sword. They say he shook the American public by his very presence. And do you know what he told me?"

This was, obviously, new to the monks who were listening to all this with wonder.

"Even there, Naren told me, 'The glory of the Master is manifest in incredible abundance. How many earnest seekers came to me and listened raptly to what I spoke about our beloved, unique Lord! Indeed, they were enchanted by the saga of his life and message! Enchanted, that is the truth!'"

Ma paused and, as if clinching her attitude to swadeshi, etc, she spoke again: "They also are my children! What do you think?"

That brought the conversation to an end.

But then Ma knows that even *her* children are not exempt from evil deeds. When Ma heard that the sister and wife of one of the devotees were made to walk all the way to a police station by the British police, Ma blazed forth in fury:

"Is this the company's order or the heroics of the police? If they continue like this, the end of their rule is not far!"

When she heard that the women were let out later, Ma made the most revelatory statement about her care, concern and compassion for her children!

"If they were not released, I could not have slept at all through the night!"

But then Mother's anger is not retaliatory but reformative. *That* is the paradox. For, if anger at the British rule could be evoked in one context, in another there is resentment but not at evil but at unwarranted discrimination.

And it happened thus.

Some garments were to be brought for Ma's nephews and nieces. One of the monastic disciples, Ishanananda, was asked to buy them. Perhaps, a strong nationalist, he brought for all of them only swadeshi clothes. Ma's children were obviously upset.

"Why did you buy such coarse clothes? They are too heavy and make us feel flustered. Please go again and bring us…."

The children said and gave a long list of the kind of clothes they liked. The Swami was obviously annoyed. "Do you think I will buy all

They Too Are My Children

that *firangi* (foreign) stuff? Nothing doing! We should buy and encourage Swadeshi goods!"

Holy Mother was sitting quietly in a corner. Serenely listening to this. Until she felt that enough was enough. Then, in gentle but firm accents, she said:

"Child! They whom you consider as foreigners, too, are my children! This house includes and is for everyone. You know I just cannot be partial to anyone. Please go and bring clothes which they would like to have."

But Ma is most sensitive and never – repeat, never – hurts the feelings of any one. She knew that her Swadeshi favouring child would feel hurt. Didn't she declare plainly and directly? "Should anyone ever utter a thing that hurts another feelings? An unpleasant truth, though true, must not be uttered. For that grows into a habit. By indulging in rude words one's nature becomes rude. One's sensitivity is lost if one has no control over one's speech. And once a man casts all consideration for others to the winds, he stops at nothing."

The Swadeshi-lover Swami corroborates this: "I observed later that Mother never called me whenever anything foreign was to be brought. It was not in mother's temperament, her nature, to hurt anyone..."

No wonder Mother can only be Mother and none else!

Chapter Six

He Would Have Drowned Himself in the Ganga

What an enchanting and enchanted life Ma and the Master had in the grounds of Dakshineswar, hallowed by their presence! Ma in that small space but now the entire world is the vast expanse of her grace! And the Master's *Kshetra*? The *punyakshetra* to which countless devotees, seekers, academically prodigal children flock! Their lives inspire and invigorate: even they who have a purely clinical concern!

Isn't it then wonderful to listen to what the one says about the other? Especially Ma's words about her Lord and Master have special charm. For the simple reason that Ma tells straight, without any façade, any narrative artifice. Everything in what she says is transparent, with the clarity of a pure crystal!

Let us meditate on what she says about Master's unique quality: his renunciation Ma describes it as his splendour. "That alone was his splendour," she said.

He Would Have Drowned Himself in the Ganga

Splendour! Yes, in every sense of the word. His physical form, his unparalleled *sadhana*, his visions, above all, his words: all are radiant with unique splendour; his *vibhuti*. If we can use the word. But this glorious, radiant being had no hierarchy. The smallest jobs were as expressive as the historic gift of "freedom from fear" to, potentially, the whole of humanity. Though the enactment was a miniature play in the Cossipore Garden House on that momentous day…

So was it in renunciation, *tyaga*. Few could equal and none has excelled him in his total disregard of possessions. The two snares of *samsara*, money and matrimony, he sacralised; money has its uses so long as it doesn't attract its fatal abuses. Then greed, gluttony, etc., will follow. As for matrimony, it is closely linked to money perhaps the link is suggested by the inclusive nature of the word itself. Matri*mon(e)*y. In this regard Thakur, again, remains unique. Matrimony is no obstacle to the quest for Mother! Mother herself has assumed all the forms; all gendered forms….

Possession is the peculiar paralytic preoccupation in our age. Consumerism has no other summit to climb: it is at its zenith and is showing its *viswarupa*, its protean form promise the paradise but propel us towards perennial perils!

That if we take as our scenario, here is the Master's play.

With his slightly faltering steps we see him going to Nahabat, Ma's – Lakshmi's – *griha*. He reaches the threshold:

"Sorry to come at this hour dear,!" he says, on the threshold:

Ma was surprised. Rarely does he come to her abode. The event could be counted on one's finger tips.

"Are you sleeping?" he asks

"No. Not at all. Tell me, Master, what brings you here at this hour!" Ma esquires.

"Nothing great. I found that my small bag is empty…"

"You mean the tiny one in which you keep the spices?"

"Yes. Exactly. I thought I could take some, if some are available."

"No problem. Here they are. You can chew them here itself, if you feel like!"

That would give Ma an opportunity to gaze at that lovely form for a few more minutes. Who would care for even darkness? Didn't the Mother tell us how, like molten gold, his body shone with unearthly splendour!

"His complexion was like the colour of gold…. It blended with the colour of the golden amulet which he wore on his arm. When I used to rub him with oil, I could clearly see a luster coming out of his entire body….. People would look at him wonder-struck when he went with slow steady steps to the Ganges to take his bath…."

No wonder Ma wants the Master to stay for a few minutes even on the pretext of chewing spices. Thakur takes the spices, pops them in… Then the idea strikes Ma:

"Here are some more. I packed them in a paper. You can take them and put them in the small bag you have…." Ma says.

We don't know what state, by then, the Master was. He says: "All right. Give it." He turns back.

Ma stands watching and wonders: "Why is he not going in the direction of his room?"

He Would Have Drowned Himself in the Ganga

Even before the thought could complete itself, she sees him going towards the embankment of the Ganga. Is he going to wash his feet? Or take a few sips?

She notices, panic stricken. With his faltering steps, he is sure to fall into the river! Oh my God! What is he doing? ... She discretely follows a few yards behind and overhears:

"Mother, shall I drown myself?" he was saying repeatedly.

He has forgotten the way to his room. And now he implores the Mother to tell him whether he should drown himself! What has happened? Did I do anything that upset him to this alarming extent?

But she heard Hriday running to his uncle. He catches hold of him and takes him back to his room. Not a minute late; that would mean the Master jumping into the lap of Mother Ganga.

Ma heaves a sigh of relief. But the nagging question asserts itself: What led him to the Ganga and not to his room? Not for long. In a flash she realizes:

"Because I placed a few spices in a paper on his hand, he lost his way and wanted to drown himself.... Such renunciation that it becomes part of the body's reflexes!"

As Ma recalls: "His renunciation was hundred per cent complete."

Chapter Seven
Here Puja Is Done Only for Her!

Evening worship was over. Sarat Maharaj oversaw the whole thing and felt joyous. Perhaps, something else stirred in his mind. He called a brahmachari:

"Child! Are you free?" he asked.

"Yes, Maharaj!"

"Then do something for me. Take this ornament to Ma, make pranams, give it to her and, take her *prasada* and come back."

The brahmachari was overjoyed that he was given such an opportunity. But he was also a bit puzzled. He thought for a minute surely the great Swami wants that the ornament should be placed before the image of Durga. Sarat Maharaj saw his hesitation, easily guessed the reason. And told him again:

"I know what you are thinking. You have to go to Ma who is in the Garden House, give this jewel to her. And don't forget to make pranams!"

Here Puja Is Done Only for Her!

And in words which annul the difference between the image of Ma and the *Chinmaya,* vibrant, presence of Mother in their midst, the most authentic biographer of the great Master declared: "Here the puja is done only for her!"

Sarat Maharaj ought to know. For didn't he declare when he wrote the *Lila Prasanga* that: "Nothing beyond my spiritual experience has been recorded in this book." Moreover, Mother praised him as her "burden-bearer!"

Do we need further assurance? The unique spiritual son of Thakur, Brahmanandaji Maharaj worshipped the Holy Mother on a Mahashtami Day with one hundred and eight lotus flowers!

Chapter Eight
Dashing Down Like an Arrow!

Strange is the divine play of the Master! And Ma never ceased to wonder at the various facets of this absorbing *Lila*. But we, who at a later date and in a changing and changed atmosphere contemplate them, are filled with varied responses. But behind all these responses what stood out for me was the Master's human and divine interplay. He is intensely human and yet inscrutably, mysteriously, superhuman.

Observe the visions: the coming of his disciples, their antecedents, indeed, the sway and sweep of his impact on the so-called "foreigners" and, the most startling of all, his revelation that his consort was already there in Jayarambati! Since the occult is suspect, we don't use the word. But then what is a miracle except an encounter between our love and the Master's / Mother's love?

Both are – if one wants one word to describe them – exemplars of love! Unconditional, therefore immeasurable, love. Whether we perceive it or not, even when we are blind and indifferent to it, their love is like

Dashing Down Like an Arrow!

the gentle breeze which, ceaselessly blowing, caresses our feverish bodies! The Holy Mother said rightly: "The Master was born on earth this time to liberate all, the rich and the poor, the learned and the illiterate. The Malaya breeze is blowing here. He who will unfurl his sail and take refuge in the Master will be blessed indeed."

It is this love which makes the Master reveal the glory and grandeur of his love by doing things which only the miracle of love can! In short, Master's love is miraculous in a way that makes him unveil unreal to us, the enormous Reality of his Being. In such contexts the ordinary laws of nature are asked to take a back seat! For the simple reason that they are his playmates.

Beloved Thakur was at Cossipore Garden House as his illness needed a cooler, pollution free area. It was on December 11, 1885 that he moved there. He was so ill that not even a drop of water could go in without causing excruciating pain. And as Ma herself said narrating the incident that happened in this condition, "The Master was then completely bed-ridden"

And how could Master, in this condition, do what he did?

One day the disciples serving him devotedly had a fancy to drink the juice of a date-palm in the garden. They wanted to tap it in the evening.

"Master is sick and bed-ridden. Let us not bother him by telling him about our plan!" declared one of the group.

The rest agreed.... Mother was doing her work in the kitchen; casually she glanced and saw something incredible:

"What is this? Master is darting down the staircase like an arrow? I can't believe this!"

She rubbed her eyes and glanced again. The eyes didn't deceive her and she was stunned.

"Is this possible? He needs help even to change sides on his bed! And he is rushing down like this! It's not an optical illusion. I'm sure. I'm seeing him with my own eyes! All right, let me check."

Ma went up and saw the bed was empty. She became alarmed and searched every nook and corner of the room and almost everywhere else. She returned to her room, confused, dismayed. She didn't know what to do. But in no time she saw something equally strange: the Master was going back to his room as speedily as he had gone out! Perhaps it took only five or at the most eight minutes for all this to happen.

Ma heaved a sigh of relief that he was safe and back in his bed. Nothing untoward had happened. But she was curious, naturally, to know what had exactly happened. She saw him later and asked:

"I saw you going down indeed, dashing down swiftly like an arrow! How come…."

Thakur interrupted her (smiling): "Oh, dear! You noticed that? And I thought none did!"

"Yes. I saw and now tell me what exactly happened," Ma said.

"All right. I will tell you. They are all youngsters. They wanted to drink the juice of the date palm tree in that corner of the garden. And they merrily went there," Master said.

"It is all right. What is odd about it? After all boys will be boys…," cut in Ma.

"Nothing wrong, yes. But I *saw* a black cobra at the foot of the tree. It is so ferocious that it would have bitten them. All of them without exception. But then they didn't know it was there. And, I *had to go* by a different route and drive it away. I did and also warned it never come here again! Now do you know why I dashed down like, as you say, an arrow?"

Mother now knew. But still puzzled. The enactment was over. Master *knew* that Ma will continue to be worried.

"Don't tell this to anyone. In fact, I myself will say it is all your imagination. Too much of cooking heightened your imagination by heating the brain!" he said, closing the subject.

Ma is Mahamaya does she not know that Master is Shiva himself? In that entrancing scene of playing the role of Shiva in Kamarpukur, he, she learnt, was seen by some as Shiva himself and worshipped. And cobra, whether black or white, is his ornament.

Who knows, he may have dashed down just to give his *darshan* to his companion, after all! And illness? How could he move from the bed? For God, anything and everything is possible. Is it not?

Above all, don't forget that epiphany on the grounds of Dakshineswar which came to his *rasaddar,* Mathur Babu. He *saw* the Master as Shiva and Shakti in the same figure! Can Thakur's *lila* have a *more* entrancing moment?

Chapter Nine
She Heard a Jingling Sound

Sushilabala was rubbing Mother's feet with oil. It was the hour of twilight. Light slowly beginning to fade into the womb of night. Perhaps, an hour that holds the human game of getting tossed between light and darkness at its peak. And as the Master was fond of singing; "In intense darkness, O Mother, Thy face sparkles!"

Mother obviously needed that small help: her feet ached quite a bit. And who knows how many of her children, prodigal or prudent, troubled them!

One recalls the devotee who knocked her head with force on her big toe! Ma cried out with pain. And the devotee explained: "I knocked the feet that touched those hallowed places, Jayarambati, Dakshineswar, Cossipore and of course Kamarpukur, not to speak of places outside – and made them holy, holy, holy…." And one is stunned by the context in which, after adoring, nay worshipping, her, Thakur himself placed all he gained at those blessed feet!

She Heard a Jingling Sound

Isn't Sushilabala immensely, incredibly lucky to be there at that moment? For being there to listen to an extraordinary revelation. The Holy Mother is, they know, generally reticent to talk about herself! But during those very moments came the revelation.

It all happened so suddenly. As if at the most appropriate moment the curtain on the most momentous truth had to be slightly drawn. Still, the revelation is shrouded in twilight. Nalini, daughter of Mother's brother, came downstairs. Impelled by cosmic forces she spoke: "Aunty, I want to ask you something!"

"All right! Go ahead and ask!" said Ma.

"Thakur is called Bhagavan and he commands respect as one. We also accept that. A Sivalinga flashed a radiant light which entered the grandma's womb," Nalini said.

Mother was listening to all this, presumably smiling. She waited.

"But, aunty, in your case, we do respect you as we do Thakur...." The voice trailed off.

Mother smiled. A disarming smile for her children and said: "Shall I tell you something! But you should remember that people say so many things. Therefore, it is better that I tell myself.

"At that time my mother was staying in my grandmother's place. She went out one day and was sitting in a distracted way under a *bilva* tree. It was then that this happened. She saw a pretty girl swinging from a tree. She was just six years old. What happened to my mother is a mystery. But she was overpowered! Perhaps, the reason could be: the pretty six-year old child came down from the tree. But my mother did not *see* the girl-child. Strangely she felt, afterwards, something enter her womb, and she lost all consciousness!"

They were all listening with rapt attention. Mother herself telling about her advent! But, then, someone asked: "Mother, we also heard that the beautiful girl was laughing and dancing atop that tree! And she soon caught your Ma Shyamasundari's neck and started swinging. Seeing this child, she became unconscious and later, after becoming conscious, she felt she was with a child! That the child entered her womb! Is this true?"

Mother nodded and added: "When people talk about such things, don't you know that according to their perception, they tell it!"

"Then what is the truth?" the person persisted.

Mother paused. It seemed too long. Then she said, clearly but almost inaudibly as if she didn't want the thing to be loud and strident: "He who is the Master, am I!"

Chapter Ten
Does She Not Know Who You Are?

The Master was severely ill. The throat was racked with pain. They said it was the clergyman's sore throat. Some suspected it could be a fatal cancer. Of course Ma was sick with fear: curtain down? Is Mother Kali taking back her child into her bosom and calling it a day for his *lila*? Ma was racked with doubts, but she knew that this was the period he needed her most. His delicate frame and constitution demanded special care which only Ma was capable of giving.

In spite of all her doubts and misgivings, the disciples in a final effort to get the Master cured, shifted him to Calcutta and finally to the Cossipore Garden House. What a name for the final lila of *this* Shiva! Kashi! It rings a bell! From Kamarpukur to Kashi! And it is in *this* Kashi that Thakur revealed himself as the summation of all gods and goddesses. Indeed, the wish fulfilling kalpavriksha, kalpa-tree, blessing all in and through his band of disciples!

But Ma had to stay back at Dakshineswar. She would have insisted – as a *sahadharmini par excellence* – that her place was with him wherever he was and in whatever condition, well or ill. Did she not rush to Dakshineswar from Jayarambati when the slightest breath of rumor that he was "mad" reached her? But she also knew that the Master took the decision. Sensitive to the subtle nuances of her Lord's nature, she was unerring in sensing what he had in his mind! In short, eager, indeed desperate, she was to be with the ailing Master at Cossipore, but it was the Master who had to decide.

Devotees, perhaps, had their own theories about her staying back in Dakshineswar, even after the Master had left. Thus it happened one day that two close women devotees started airing their own views. Golap-Ma, a close companion of Ma, asked another equally intimate devotee: "Yogin! Do you know why Thakur didn't ask Ma to accompany him to Cossipore?"

"How do we know? Master has, you know, his own reasons. If he wanted he would have certainly asked her to be in Cossipore to serve him!" Yogin-Ma said with, one can imagine, slight annoyance.

"That is precisely what I, too, am saying. Perhaps, there is a reason for this, some basis for this!"

"And, pray, what is that?" asked Yogin-Ma.

"I don't know but I guess Master was angry with Ma and left Dakshineswar for that reason and went away to Calcutta!"

"Master *angry* with Ma? The One who did not even address her as *Tu* but always *aap*? Is it conceivable?" Yogin-Ma almost cried.

"I know all that. But I think he *was* angry!"

"OK. If you say so!"

Does She Not Know Who You Are?

But Yogin-Ma was puzzled – if not rattled. She felt she couldn't contain herself. Ma should know, so she went and told her.

The effect was devastating. Her Lord angry with her? Was it possible? If so, did she commit any serious mistake, serious to the extent of *making him leave* his beloved Bhavatarini and blessed Ganga and Dakshineswar? He was sick, but sick with anger against her?

Tears welled up. Ma started weeping inconsolably. But, in the midst of that uncontrollable grief, she quickly decided that she must go and ask the Master. And, if she did commit a mistake, he would certainly forgive her. She immediately got into a carriage and rushed to Calcutta.

Alighting, Ma rushed to Thakur's presence and straight away asked him: "You have come away here, being angry with me, haven't you?"

The Master was aghast. He angry with her? Not even the trace of being angry with his beloved Sarada crossed his mind. Let alone, making it the reason to come away to Calcutta!

He spoke firmly: "No! No! Who told you that I was angry? Who concocted this story? Tell me!"

Ma must have heaved a sigh of relief. There was nothing to be agitated. Her Lord is an ocean of love and compassion. He cannot be angry with her. But he must know who said such a thing.

"Golap said that," Ma told the Master.

Thakur was furious. The alleged anger at Ma that was the reason for leaving Dakshineswar now became real! And directed to Golap: "Golap, of all people! Is this true? She spoke like that and made you weep?"

Ma saw her Lord livid with anger. Rare for her to see such anger in her Lord. Intense, indescribable love alone could bring such anger, anger that the loved one was hurt, reducing her to tears! And hurt by allegations made by Golap who ought to know!

"Does she not know who you are?" Thakur thundered. "Where is Golap? Let her see me! I'll tell her never to concoct such stories and you can be assured I won't spare anyone in such things!"

Ma was totally relieved. Yes, it cannot be otherwise. Imagine she making him angry!

Golap *did* see the Master again. The Master scolded her severely. The question is why severely? The answer is in the very revelatory words Master spoke: "What did you tell her to make her not only get upset but upset to the extent of weeping? And rushing to me? *Do you not know who she is?*"

Golap knew what was coming and was almost on the verge of tears: "Forgive me! Master!! I didn't realize what I was saying!"

"Golap! You know something? If I get angry, I doesn't matter. If your Ma gets angry, even I cannot save you! Go this instant and seek her forgiveness!"

Golap rushed to the Mother. As usual Ma was sitting serene and tranquil. She saw Golap weeping and agitated: "Dear! Tell me what's the matter?"

"Mother! I am rushing here from our Master! He was awfully angry with me. I didn't realize the enormity of the things I was saying. I merely blurted out those words! I didn't mean them! Please forgive me!"

Mother remained silent and smiling. She didn't speak a word. But patted on Golap's back and merely uttered her name: "Oh Golap!" The gesture did magic; Golap's worry vanished, as if touched by a magic wand!

Chapter Eleven
I Cannot Forget the Child!

Mother was worried. Actually envious. One may wonder, even our Holy Mother gets worried? She and the Master embody the pinnacle of renunciation and detachment. How can they get worried or anxious? The wonder is: they do. The interplay of the human and the divine is the most fascinating aspect of their nature.

Mother was worried because Maku's son was critically ill. (Maku was one of the daughters of Mother's brothers, Prasanna Kumar). Ever since Ma got the news that he was sick, she was filled with intense agony. The child was ailing in Jayarambati. That doubled the agony.

Ma called Brahmachari Varada and told him: "Varada! See to it that a palanquin is kept ready. Perhaps, the boy will survive. In that case, I shall go and see him in the morning. But then how to get news so early?"

"Don't get worried, Mother," Mahindra who was there said, "we shall go very early in the morning and get the news."

Mother knew that the news was not going to be good. Death always is a mystery but not for a *jnani*. They are constantly aware that birth has to end in death: they are indissolubly linked. But then grief is also inevitable. That is the strange thing about death: none wants to face it but everyone has to. As the poet said, since we do not wait for death, death kindly waits for us! And the alive who grieve for the dead are themselves dead in due or mid course!

But Ma's worry is different. It is not born out of attachment rooted in delusion. It is born out of the right kind of attachment. An attachment which neutralizes the negative consequences of attachment so that one grieves without that grief being a source of bonding! As Prabodh Babu, a devotee, who saw Mother shedding torrential tears at the death of Dwaraknath Majumdar says, "No doubt tears came out of her eyes but I could clearly understand that it was bereft of attachment in the worldly sense."

But things happened swiftly. A swami came back from Jayarambati. Mother immediately guessed: "What happened, Vaikuntha?"

All present remained silent. They were too overwhelmed with grief to inform Ma. Then Ma asked: "You don't need to tell me. He passed away. But when?"

"At half-past five, Ma!" One can imagine Ma's response. Her love encompassed Maku's son as it did everyone. She queried again: "Shall I go now and see…."

"No use, Ma. The dead body has been removed straightaway …." Vaikuntha told her.

Instantly Ma began crying in a way that rent the heart of everyone with a grief that was unbearable. Ma's crying was so intense that they couldn't

I Cannot Forget the Child!

but be deeply moved seeing it. And strangely, even when she stopped for a few minutes, grief overtook her again and she plunged into crying again.

What a heart-rending scene! And what warmth and humane concern! Ma is not one of those dry-as-dust Advaitins for whom everything is Maya and therefore grief and sorrow traps that Maya sets! Ma herself declared: "If you love any human being you have to suffer for it. He is blessed who loves God alone. There is no suffering in loving God."

We get here the clue that unlocks the reason for Ma's intense grief for that boy. For, the boy had uncommon devotion! Uncommon for that age. One recalls what Ma herself told: "I can't tell you how intelligent that boy was! I clearly remember something that he did which deeply touched me. Maku and the boy were about to go to Jayarambati. And do you know what he did? He gathered a few flowers – wild roses – and came to me. With touching innocence and devotion he placed them at my feet! And said: 'Auntie! Don't you see how beautiful they look!'"

Then he did something more, something which must have been impelled by innate *samskaras*:

"He bowed down, prostrated to me and took the dust of my feet! Then he picked up some, put them reverentially in his pocket. After this only he left for Jayarambati!"

As if giving the reason for this unusual behavior, Ma said something she does rarely and that prophetically: "Perhaps, some devotee in his former birth has been born as this boy. And this *must have been his last birth*. You cannot otherwise explain the expert way in which he used to do puja at the age of three! Three! Imagine!"

Must have been his last birth! How wonderfully this prophetic power parallels Thakur's own affirmation of his direct disciples as his companions in other yugas and other forms! Ma *knew* everything but camouflaged that knowledge! She willingly suspended manifestation of her true nature. Aren't we therefore grateful to this dear boy who contextually impelled Ma to make this revelation? Ma is perfect in designing a scene. But what about her grief?

"I brought him up and the loss is irreparable, terrible, to me!"

What love and compassion! The wonder is not just for that boy who, presumably, did lot of *punya,* but for everyone whether they know it or not, accept it or not! Perhaps, we can end this episode by recalling what she does, among other things, for her initiated but errant chelas.

Mother, an attendant noticed, was doing *japa* late at night. He was surprised and asked why she should do such a thing. Ma revealed the reason: "I am helpless, child! My children come and are eager for initiation. They almost entreat me. But do you know what they do? They take the Mantra and go, merrily. And they don't do *Japa*. Most irregularly. Perhaps not even once."

The attendant was listening, almost aghast.

Ma said something more: "But as I have shouldered their burden should I not look after them? That's why I do japa…" and added the most revelatory hint: "Not just that. I pray to the Master: 'Lord! Grant them enlightenment. Grant them emancipation, and do assume their responsibility here and hereafter.'"

Today we are stunned and slowly tears well up in our eyes: it is not Maku's son alone, *we are* all your children and many of us are prodigal, even 'profligate', but do have compassion, continuing to succor us, nourish us!

Chapter Twelve
Mere Play of Mahamaya

Once a disciple asked the Mother: "Ma! Do you always remember your real nature?"

What he wanted to know is what exactly all of us want to know. Seeing the way in which she immersed herself in "ordinary" work, we all get that doubt. Moreover, since comparison with the Master is inevitable, how come she rarely goes into samadhi, as Father did? She was, of course, concealing her real nature, her *sahaja prakriti*, we tell ourselves. Perhaps, the real reason could be: humans cannot bear to see the *virat rupa*, the cosmic form of Ma!

"How can I always remember my true nature? That would put an end to my normal work. And could I do all these duties?" Ma replied.

In other words, *Samsara* pulls her from *Nirvana*, if one wants to put it that way. But Ma adds something more by way of clarification: "…even in the midst of my various activities, whenever I wish, I can understand by the slightest effort that all this is the *mere play of Mahamaya!*"

"Whenever I wish," Ma says. Ma's wish depends on the context and the need. It is her *Iccha*. Then *Jnana* and *Kriya* shaktis blend to show us that *real nature* which she embodies.

Ma clarifies in another way in another context. When she says: "The excessive manifestation of divinity; do you know what it does? It creates fear in the minds of devotees. They cannot feel intimate!"

Not just fear but, often, terror. As we saw in the case of Harish. But that was just a solitary incident. There were quite a few where the *Roudra rupa,* the terrifying form of Ma manifested Itself.

One was concerned with the land on which the Master's temple was to be constructed in Kamarpukur. It was something concerning the Zamindar of Kamarpukur, Lahababu. Lahababu consented secretly, in connivance with Shibudada's wife, to give away her daughter in marriage. Even Ma was kept in the dark about this and the fact that the girl was ultimately saved from the undesirable marriage. Obviously, the Zamindar was angry. A devotee, Prabodh, said in a careless manner about the construction of the proposed temple being affected: "Does it matter if Thakur's temple is not constructed on that piece of land? He has so many temples and he is not, certainly, waiting for this temple to come up."

Ma was listening to all this manifestly unhappy: "How can you talk like that, Prabodh! You are not aware of what you are saying! Kamarpukur is *Mahapithasthana,* a sacred pilgrim place. And you are so careless in saying that it doesn't matter!" said Ma.

Prabodh persisted: "Shibudada's wife will boil with anger and even set fire to the place!"

Mother's patience, perhaps, reached its point of no return: with uncommon bite in her voice she said, "All right! Let it happen just like that! Let it happen! Good! Everything is Thakur's will. If it is His will, let it happen! *I know he liked cremation grounds and then everything will become a huge cremation ground!*"

And Ma began to laugh! And others mistaking it as amused laughter joined in and laughed. Then it happened. The eye-witness Prabodh tells: "We joined in the laughter but we had done so but for only two or three seconds when *all of a sudden her laughter* became louder and louder!"

Continuing the story of the extraordinary incident, Prabodh notes: "It became louder and louder and fearful and went on increasing gradually for twenty to twenty-five seconds. *In that voice everyone else's was overpowered and drowned…*"

Laughter that makes the worlds tremble as Ma tramples them under her feet. If the Master was fond of cremation grounds so is Ma, the Smashana Kali! She will, if she wills, reduce everything to dust! Can't she? She can, and she does. Proof!

Those were the First World War days. As was her nature, Ma took keen interest in everything around her. She knew the tremendous upheavals going on in various parts of the globe. And, in this case, Ma asked a devotee: "Dear! They say a world war is going on. Can you bring a paper and read out the news of the war?"

The devotee brought the paper and read out many things. Golap-Ma and Yogin-Ma also were there, quite near the Mother. Obviously, they too were listening. Perhaps, they were wondering why Ma was taking interest in worldly matters. Didn't the Master say that they should not take interest in newspapers?

Ma was listening to the huge destruction that the war involved. Hundreds of men and women, she heard, were killed. This was news that had an unexpected impact on the Mother. A distinct change appeared. It was incredible, knowing her usually tranquil, unruffled mood. There was something unnamably fierce.

In the beginning Ma's voice was muted, low-key: 'ha…ha.' In no time the pitch was shrill, the voice fearful, terrible with the "ha…ha," reaching the zenith. It created a din so terrible that Ma's high voice shook the entire building for full two minutes.

What a scene! The Holy Mother so gentle, like the gentle dew that drops unknown and unheard, shaking a whole building with her terrible voice? It doesn't fit in with her image. But Ma is also the fierce Kali who breaks the brains of countless children of hers and dances in ecstasy….

The scene was nerve-racking, filling the hearts of those present with a fear that froze them. But Golap-Ma and Yogin-Ma quickly recovered. They approached the Mother and prayed: "Oh Mother of the Universe! We cannot bear to see your *Ugra-rupa,* your fierce form. Bless us with your *Sowmya-rupa,* your gentle form!"

Slowly Ma assumed her normal form. The fierce form was effaced like a line drawn on water disappears! Mahamaya does not frighten us beyond what we can bear!

Recall the dacoits "parents" who escorted Ma through the most dangerous place to Dakshineswar? What did the cutthroat dacoits see in

Mere Play of Mahamaya

Ma to become so docile? We need not speculate. Ma herself wondered and asked them: ("Why are you showering so much affection on me?")

And they said something most revelatory: "You are not an ordinary person! We saw you as Ma Kali!"

Ma was surprised: "What are you talking? What have you seen?"

After all, though branded as dacoits, they were also her parents. And can parents hide something or say a fib in fun to a child, to a daughter like Ma? They firmly said: "Yes. We have, indeed, seen Kali! Perhaps, because we are dacoits our daughter is hiding this from us!"

After this, who doesn't want to be even dacoit parents?

Ma into dacoits and drunkard.

Thou dost reveal

Thy Form scaled

from the devout!

Chapter Thirteen
White for the Master, Yellow for Me

Ma once observed: "It is only by accepting an illusion that I am so. This is nothing but continuing in the illusion." Extraordinarily meaningful words. What does Mother mean by "I am so?" That she appears as an ordinary woman involved with everything that such a woman usually – in India – does. That seems to be the meaning. If this is an illusion, Ma cannot continue to be an ordinary woman – giving that illusion – unless the illusion continues.

The thing is: She willingly *accepts* the illusion. Like the Upanishadic analogy has it: Mahamaya, like the spider, weaves her own web and gets caught in it! For sport, for fun. It is all Ma's *lila*, says the Master. But we generally observe it in the Master but slip when we come to the Mother. Since the Master himself declared the oneness which exists between Bhavatarini in the temple, his own mother and his consort, there can be little doubt about who Ma Saradadevi is. Not just a hint, but the Master *showed* it in a way.

White for the Master, Yellow for Me

Recall that incident in which the Master was walking on the grounds of Dakshineswar. His *rasaddar* Mathur Babu watched him unobserved: in one direction he saw Shiva in another, Shakti, Mahamaya! And did Mathur or we realize that the Master was registering in his own body the identity between Himself and His divine consort and what he showed to Mathur was Ma herself as the other side, an extension, of himself! After all, She was, as the hymn puts it Ramakrishna *gathaprana!*

The question is: did the Mother at any time concede this. Plainly, without any ambiguity, without any subterfuge?

Yes, she did, and in this way, at Jayarambati in January 1919.

Mother was standing in an unusually expressive way. We already saw that to redeem the deranged Harish she took the form of Bagala (and in one version, she even put out her tongue like Ma Kali!) This time we do not know the exact reason. Except that there entered in the Mother a rare impulse – *spandana* – to shed the Maya – illusion – and sport in her own Form.

The *iccha* triggered *bhava*. And in a split second she stood in the form of Kali, what is more: showing *Vara* and *Abhaya mudras*. The esoteric gestures of giving a boon and offering protection, freedom form fear. "Shed all fear!" the gestures proclaim – "I am here only to give you *abhaya.*"

Did anyone witness this? Any most fortunate being? Yes. There was. One Naresh Chakravorty. We do not know how he took in the scene. But it is certain that he desired to offer worship to Ma. It is obviously through Ma's grace he saw Her Kali form and yet retained his wits to ask her, "May I offer worship to you, Ma?"

Ma accepted! *That* is the miracle! And how unusual that she did something else: "Yes. You can. And I will also tell you what flowers to offer! Bring both white and yellow flowers. Do you know why? The white are for Thakur. You know, He likes White. And I like Yellow ones. Can you get them?"

Of course Chakravorty did. If it is Ma's – the *Paramaprakritis* – wish, the entire cosmos, everything in it, bends in adoration and offers whatever she desires! The flowers came and Ma said: "Child! Place the white flowers on my right foot and the yellow ones on my left one!"

Chakravorty did as directed. And we find here one parallel. Just as Mathur found Shiva and Shakti in Thakur here Ma shows Herself on the left – and shows the Master on the right! And here Ma didn't move this way or that way or to and fro! She just stood and what more forms Chakravorty saw is anybody's guess. We who, in point of time, come later can only pray:

Ma, show us, if possible, only your *Sowmya rupa,* your benign form. We, poor mortals pray and crave for your love which you give unasked and unconditional and thereby set us free from all fear!

Chapter Fourteen
Why Not?

One of the most mysterious facets in the lives of incarnations is the incongruity between themselves and their families. For instance, Sri Rama had Kaikeyi, Krishna had his uncle Kamsa. And so on. We don't know why they grace such families. Logic does not help. Theology offers explanations but Ma offers the most convincing one.

A disciple brought the mail. One was about one of her disciple's death. Ma remarked on the universal phenomenon: "All must die. It is good that this one died in Banaras, the holiest of cities. Rather than die in a pool or the bank of a lake!"

Somewhat detached, almost clinical Ma appears. But then she is Ma of both genesis and dissolution.

There were also letters from her brothers. Ma listened while they were being read and remarked: "I know what they write about. They want money and more money. And also about how they quarreled with each other! Nothing more nothing less!" She once candidly said: "Look at my own relatives see the evil company I am in!"

The disciple was obviously unhappy. Why should relations of Ma suffer? Can't they be helped? With a mere wish she can order, indeed, create anything. Compassion filled the disciple and he made a request on their behalf: "Ma! Why don't you see to it that they get plenty of money? We know you can. Also, please tell the Master about it. Let them, Ma, enjoy the material life and reach the point of satiety. Then they will not pester you further."

Pat came Ma's reply: "Will they ever be satisfied? Nothing can satisfy them. It is not in their nature. They are like other worldly persons. Are they ever satiated with enjoyments? And, besides, they are extremely good at spinning out stories of sorrow and suffering…"

The disciple, perhaps, was seeing a different dimension of the Holy Mother. He must have been amazed at the way in which Ma was making a point often bypassed: worldliness, the unending thirst for enjoyment hardly exempts anyone. Even they who are related by ties of blood to incarnations! Another striking example, we know, is Hriday, Master's nephew – constant companion and protector. He had to, in the last days of his life, eke out a living selling clothes from door to door!

"Look at *my* brothers!" Ma continued: "It is Kali who constantly wants money! Now another brother Prasanna is following his footsteps and makes constant demands for money and more money. Only my other brother Varada never asks. He is sensible and says, 'Where will sister get money from?'"

Why Not?

The disciples must have been puzzled. As we are now. The family is strange. The Incarnation of all goddesses getting pestered by a family of such brothers! Incredible and incongruous: (And of course, the insane sister-in-law does not ask. Not that she doesn't want, but because she is insane!) Racked by such doubts, the disciple asked a question which all of us, at one time or the other, asked ourselves: "Then, Ma, why were *you* born in *that* family?"

Ma answered instantly, without pausing, "Why not? My parents were very good, upright people. A staunch devotee of Rama, my father led an ideal Brahmin's life. Unlike what the Master called rice and plantain bundling Brahmins, he never accepted gifts – *dakshina* – indiscriminately. But don't imagine he was one of those killjoy, austere Brahmins. He loved to smoke. And so innocent and humble that he called any passerby in a friendly way and invited him: "Come in, *bhai*, have a smoke!"

Why not? Yes. The answer is implicit in the very cosmos Ma creates. Is it not "of mingled yarn, good and ill together?" Nature, *prakriti*, balances things: Ma, as an insightful one said, does not *change* evil, she merely *chastises* it! With every incarnation, or else, the world should become progressively better! Nothing like it has happened or will happen!

If this is the design, should not Ma's own family be its miniature paradigm?

Chapter Fifteen

When You Say She Will be Cured, She Shall be Cured!

Four kinds of devotees, says the *Gita,* seek God: the afflicted, the curious, the affluence-desiring and the enlightenment-seeking ones. Of these the afflicted are plenty. Humans face all kinds of problems and naturally seek their solution or dissolution. But whether through their supplication they really get rid of their troubles is a moot question. Sometimes they do; quite often they do not. We have an analogy in Thakur's life: When his dearest and the most distinguished disciple, Swamiji, asked him to remove the acute poverty they were experiencing, the Master directed him to Bhavatarini. He knew Narendra would not ask such things of the blessed Mother. But he *did assure him* that Naren's family would have all that is needed for a decent life.

Naturally, we are curious: what about Ma?

It was a bright, sunny day. Four o'clock in the evening. Ma was relatively free from her usual load of work. A devotee came to tell Mother: "Ma! A European lady has been waiting for a long time to have your *darshan*. What should we tell her?"

When You Say She Will be Cured ...

A *European* lady for Ma's *darshan?* Quite intriguing. Isn't it? Ma never traveled abroad, knew little of Europe – as far as we know – and one can hardly expect a lady from there to seek her *darshan*. How did the lady know about Ma? There is no media coverage, as now. But as the Master said, when the flower blossoms bees come of their own accord! And the miracle of love spreads its enfolding wings far and wide. It seeks out every seeker and ensures that the seeking is not distracted by any kind of obstacle. If, as we say, all this is 'divinely' designed and is in the *blueprint*.

Ma said: "Yes. I am free. Please bring her in."

The European lady entered respectfully. I always wonder how Ma could instantly tune to allegedly foreign devotees. She didn't know their language(s), their customs and conventions. Yet there was instant rapport. The simple reason is: Ma is the Mother of all and how could she not feel perfectly at home with any and every child of hers....?

In this case Ma went a step ahead. As the lady bowed to her, Ma restrained her and, instead, "clasped her hand as one does in shaking hands." What a marvelous scene for us to contemplate! The lady trying to follow the Hindu convention of bowing down but the Mother shaking hands in the Western way! Ma doesn't talk about East-West synthesis. She simply clasped the hand and behind that clasp is the unique warmth of universal love that envelops everyone in her embrace. It was not a gesture of social etiquette but a glorious symbol of Mother's intense affection for a child of hers. Also, one can certainly argue that Ma knew how to behave in tune with time and circumstances. The Master himself advised her in this regard. But more than all these were involved in this incident.

Ma clasping the lady's hand is all the more unique. For one reason: the lady knew Bengali and knew the conventions. Accordingly, Ma now did the conventional gesture: touched the visitor's chin affectionately. Clasping the hand, caressing the chin. Both cultural specifics came together!

Then Ma asked: "What brings you here, dear?"

"Before telling you that, Ma I hope I haven't inconvenienced you by my coming!"

"No not all. Do tell me what made you come to me?"

The lady felt assured and told Ma: "Mother, I have been waiting a long time to see you. I have a problem and it is my daughter. She is critically ill. My only daughter, she is an extremely well-behaved child. One seldom finds these days such a good-natured girl. In these days many are vicious and evil-minded. That *I know*. But my child is totally different. Now she is seriously ill. I came to seek your blessings for her. Please shower your grace on her, Ma! She is my only daughter!"

Ma obviously was deeply moved and touched. Didn't she herself declare: "I can't contain myself when one draws near and calls me Mother." And again, "The purpose of one's life is fulfilled only when one is able give joy to another."

No wonder, Ma spontaneously assured: "I *shall* pray for your daughter. She will be cured."

With fervent faith, the lady said: "Mother, when *you* say that my daughter will be cured, she *shall* be cured."

Not once, but three times the devout European lady repeated this. Faith is strange and mysterious. It is inherent not acquired. And "it bloweth

When You Say She Will Be Cured ...

where it listeth." What the lady must have known of Ma to declare that what *Ma wills shall come to pass* is anybody's guess. But she already knew as a fact that faith moves mountains. Perhaps, for that reason, Ma did something else besides pray for her daughter.

Presumably Golap-Ma was watching what was happening. Ma turned to her and said: "Will you bring a flower from the altar? Please bring a lotus."

Golap-Ma brought one. Mother took it in her hand and did in the lady's presence itself what she said she would: she closed her eyes for a few moments, then looked intently at the image of her Lord and Master Sri Ramakrishna. Then she gave the lotus to the lady and asked her to touch her daughter's head with it. The European lady took it with folded hands and again bowed down before the Mother.

"I can't say, Ma, how grateful I'm! But tell me what shall I do with the flower later?" she asked.

Look at the slowly emerging scenario. Mother said I shall pray (to Thakur, of course) and she did. But why did she give a flower – a specially chosen lotus – besides? Should there also be instructions about what should be done with the flower? Was Mother doing things because, being omniscient, she knew that, unknown to herself, the lady needed a tangible, concrete thing. That, in this case, seems certain from what the lady already did, earlier in a parallel context. Hence the question: what should she do with the flower?

Mother replied: "When the flower dries up, throw it into the Ganges!"

"No, no! I cannot discard it. It is God's. I shall prepare a small bag with a piece of new cloth and keep the flower in it. I shall touch my daughter's head with it – everyday," said the lady.

Ma was, again, moved by her faith. And now came the story which explains why Ma gave a flower. The European lady revealed what she did before coming to Ma:

Ma! God, the Supreme Reality, exists. There is no doubt about that. But when my daughter was down with fever I prayed to God. My grief was unbearable. So I told God but first I kept a hanky on the table and said: 'God! I know you exist but I want proof, a tangible, concrete one!' And God gave me the proof: after quite a bit of time; I was taken aback when I found three sticks in the folds of the handkerchief! I touched my daughter with those and she got cured!

The anonymous lady was overcome with intense feeling and tears trickled down, even as she finished talking about her experience. Isn't it because she is of a nature which wants a tangible proof that Ma gave her a lotus and instruction about how to use it? Perhaps, the European streak explains this strong urge for "concrete" proof.

The lady left and did what Ma wanted her to do with the lotus. The child got cured. Deeply impressed by the lady's devotion, Ma asked her to come again, saying that she was highly pleased with her. And when the lady came, Ma gave her the greatest jewel among her many gifts: initiation. And initiation is, indeed, the core of Ma's miracle of love.

One may wonder why a lotus? Because, perhaps, one should live in the world like a dewdrop on a lotus leaf with unshakable faith in God. The dewdrop is on the lotus leaf but is not attached to it. Like a mudfish, as Thakur's image suggests. But did the lady realize that God Himself in Ma's form cured the daughter and initiated her?

Chapter Sixteen
It Has Become Mischievous

Context decides Ma's responses. What she says in one context may be at variance in another. That is the charm about her teachings. Variety of responses because of variation in contexts. Not just that Absolute miracle! It shows Ma's strategies of running the world of contingent reality and world of its transcendence.

Lunch time. At Ma's Jayarambati. 'Joyram': wherever there is Ma, there can only be joy all around. Baburam Maharaj – Subodhanandaji – and others were taking food. Jovial together! To be in Ma's place and taking her *prasada*. Is it a small thing! *Prasad* not in a temple but in the very habitat of the Mother of the cosmos.

Suddenly, a cat darted from somewhere and straight went to snatch something from Khoka Maharaj's plate. Maharaj instantly hit the cat. It was quite like a reflex. But Premananadaji was shocked. He exclaimed, visibly annoyed: "Khoka! Oh my God! You have done something shocking! Hitting a cat? Don't you know Ma assumes various forms? And this is her own place! You shouldn't have done that, Khoka!"

Mother heard about this. The whole episode was narrated by Baburam Maharaj. But, perhaps, he was least expecting Ma's response. She smiled and said: "Khoka has done nothing wrong. Indeed, he did the right thing. Something needed. Of late, the cat has become highly mischievous. It needed a spank! Yes, it did."

We wonder. In another context when someone beat a cat, Mother said, "To steal is its dharma." And asked, "Who is there always to feed it lovingly?" Here we get the clue. The cat, whom Mother fed regularly, or perhaps instructed someone "to feed it regularly," if in spite of that is mischievous and tries to steal food, it deserves slapping.

This is a lesson in love and caring. You help someone but if he or she wants to be helped continually and not do something to help himself or herself then it is using and exploiting the care and concern of another. Like you are a doormat and people rub their shoes simply because it is there and not because you really need to wipe! Mother does, as she herself affirmed, "dwell in the cat," too. But, then, the manifestation is according to *samskaras*. And if they happen to be negative, they have to be checked. Love is not saying 'yes' to anything and everything. Love involves saying 'no', too, if the context warrants. The Mother's spirituality is not a goody-goody emotive do-goodism. It is firm, and takes the context into account.

The Mother's attitude to her niece Radhu is a typical case. Ma looked after her with amazing care but at one point she made it plain that enough is enough. The girl had to be freed from dependence!

And note, too, when an insect was sought to be saved from singeing its wings, in a flame, Mother categorically said: "Kill it! Kill it! No need to have pity on it!" Strangely, when a centipede got killed by Sarat Maharaj, Ma exclaimed: "What fortune to get killed at the hands of a sadhu." Mysterious are the ways of Ma.

Chapter Seventeen
Beings All over the Universe Are My Children

They come in all shapes and sizes. And for various reasons some are curious; they hear about Ma from someone and go to see her. Most often with pet notions of their own about holy people. But, surprisingly, to them Mother makes most revelatory statements. The persons in that situation do not understand and precisely for that reason Ma seems to make such statements. Their innocence (sometimes irreverence even) is the cause and we are the beneficiaries.

It was afternoon. A disciple, Kshirodbala Roy was with the Mother. She noticed that somewhat suddenly, Ma became serious, "assumed a solemn attitude." Solemn, serious? Was Ma arranging a scene where her playful exterior – often manifest – had to be concealed? We wonder. But no need to wonder, if we contemplate what followed.

A widow arrived. To have darshan of Ma. But a widow who seemed a bit of a show-off as a great spiritual person: she wore a cloth painted with the names of Gods, a common enough insignia in many pilgrim centres. Often a cloak, too, for enjoying special privileges. And besides, she had a rosary of basil leaves adorning her neck.

Ma, obviously, noticed all this and she saw her approaching to do pranams. Instantly Ma said: "Don't touch my feet. Salute me by touching the floor. That's enough."

Did Ma guess something unsavory about the visitor? Guess? A wrong word. She knew: behind that exterior of a rosary and a cloth carrying names of Gods was an unhealthy mind. Evident, for us, in the way the widow responded to the Mother's instruction. She touched the feet and saluted! Oh my God! As we note already, feet sanctified by the radiant, celestial touch of her Lord and Master, Ramakrishna! Can all and sundry touch them? "In seeing the Mother," devotees attest, "they had actually seen Mother Kali Herself"! How dare everyone touch the feet of this Bhavatarini?

No wonder, at this stage of the enactment unfolding itself, the widow's eyes fell on the photograph of the Master. She exclaimed: "Oh my! How beautiful, how radiant it is! Do you see?"

Obviously, the question was addressed to the devotee. Kshirodbala must have had an embarrassing moment. Perhaps, she guessed that Ma's solemnity forebode something unusual. Was Ma upset by what the widow visitor was saying and doing? Yes: she forbade her to touch her feet but disregarding it, she touched her feet. And now her remarks about the photo! Ma turned to the devotee and queried.

"What do you show her?" and turning to the visitor said: "She worships him to whose photo you are pointing!"

Beings All over the Universe Are My Children

The widow found the photo beautiful. But did she know what lay beyond that beauty, something which sustained worship! Obviously, she didn't. And Ma didn't say who the person in that photo was. That dimension eluded the widow. And she fell back upon something ready at hand in the room. Pointing to the devotee, she asked Ma: "Is she your daughter?" What a question! And, besides, what for did the widow with Tulsi beads and painted holy cloth come? For eliciting details which are absolutely irrelevant. Obviously. But is it an irrelevant question? Not when we grasp Ma's answer: "Yes, my child."

Even in English (I do not know much of Bengali) the answer is intriguing. To say the least. Was Ma identifying Kshirodbala as her child – "Yes, she is my child" – or is she addressing the curious questioner, "Yes, my child, the devotee you are seeing is my child." In one case, it does refer to the devotee. In another, it could be the widow: "Yes, since you are a child or rather childish, you are putting such questions."

But then the widow took it literally. Hence the next question: "How many children have you?"

We laugh at the innocence behind the question. But should we? After all, even Ma's mother regretted that Ma had no children – of her own! Here is the trap: simple words, such splendour of meaning and significance. "Given birth to?" "How many?" – the language of measurable, quantifiable reality which is Maya, Mahamaya. And Mahamaya Herself answers: "Beings all over the universe are my children!"

But the widow was not satisfied. She repeats the question with a tag this time: "How many children have you given birth to?"

Obviously, the widow was not used to this kind of reply. Here is the trap. Our language depends on measurable, quantifiable reality. That is, where even when Mahamaya Herself reveals the enormous truth of Her advent as Ma Sarada – as herself – do we perceive it? As the widow asks, we may not ask but we entertain the same idea. She asked: "How many children have you given birth to?"

Strangest dialogue! The devotee who knows and the pretentious widow who does not know the terrifying truth of what she is seeking to know. In between is Ma balancing both: they who know and they who are deluded. But Ma is, in any sense, Ma. That is why she tells: "My husband is a man of renunciation!"

Answers which led to further questions. The widow tried to raise them. Ma reached the limit. She turned to Kshirodbala and directed her to "explain things;" she did, as clearly as possible and almost chiding her, said: "If you had known or get to know even a little about Ma, you wouldn't dare to put such questions!"

Even then the visitor was bursting with further questions. She tried to project a link saying that her daughter knew Ma. Ma cut short the episode and the widow left. Ma then directed Kshirodbala to bring some water and wash her feet. "Fan me a little," she added.

What intrigues one is the incongruous, the discrepant way things unfolded. "Beings all over the universe are my children!" – the most stunning truth said to one who could hardly comprehend it. But, for that matter, do we?

Chapter Eighteen
Let Me Not Grow

"Let me not grow,

Leaving behind the beauty of childhood!"

Yes, we, children of Ma, wouldn't like to grow and leave her lap. Or, rather we like to grow in her lap! Ma is willing, indeed, eager that we shouldn't leave the cozy comfort of her heart. But, a little we grow and that is enough for us to think that we know better! Ma tolerates our pranks and our antics. And after life's fitful fever "she lifts us into her lap, again. Again, again and again until we realize there is no gain in losing her! What she is eager to give – even begging and beseeching us to accept – we spurn. And paradoxically, beg again. Mother is never surprised. For, she knows that her toys are made to be more attractive than the Maker Herself. The granny doesn't want us to touch her. Then the *lila* is over! That *she* doesn't like. Fun and frolic in playing, not in ringing down the curtain!

The house was quiet. Varanasi. Ma was resting. And the others too retired leaving Ma some breathing space! But strangely that was not to be. The silence that enveloped the place was gently broken. A song was heard from the verandah, not loud or strident but muted, persuasive but somewhat interrogatively sad:

Where has my Mother gone?

For many days have not seen you,

Mother, take me on Thy lap

What sort of Mother art Thou,

so stony-hearted towards the child;

Grant Thy vision, Mother,

and make me weep no more!

What a heart-rending prayer! And sung exactly at the very place where the question 'where art thou' gets an answer! Affirming the Master's assurance: intense longing – *vyakulata* – weeping for Ma will instantly bring her. And there was, in this case, too intense weeping by the singer! There was no need as the song appeals for mere vision. Mother was there in her radiant physical form.

Even for us just to read the lines tugs at our heart. Though only intermittently we also cry for Ma. Then will it not tug at Ma's heart? She woke up suddenly: "Someone is singing. We should go and see, come," she told the devotee there. They went and what they saw was amazing. A girl was singing with tears pouring down uninterruptedly. What followed was much more surprising:

As the Mother sat, the girl prostrated to her and said: "Ma! Today my life-long desire is fulfilled. It is impossible for me to tell you how much joy is flooding my heart! A rare sense of well-being suffuses me!"

Ma blessed the girl and enquired about her. Ma realized that, though a beggar, the deeply devout girl was able to live fairly well. Ma said: "From what you told me I am happy that you are all right…."

But the girl intervened: "Everything about my needs is taken care of Ma. But I have one worry. I want Bhakti, devotion, of your lotus feet. Bless me with that Ma!"

We wonder: how did this beggar girl know about Ma! Not only know but was also certain that for devotion she should come to Ma? Who told her? And how did she locate the place and with her soul-stirring song make "the empress of Kailash" awake from her siesta? Miraculously, the theme of the song she sang and her own longing blended in a rich harmony that struck a responsive chord in Ma!

And what was Mother's response? Clear, unambiguous, vastly reassuring: *"Certainly you will get devotion, child!* Don't you live in the holy place where Shiva and Annapurna are eager to liberate everyone who dwells here? Their grace is there fully on you! Never have a doubt!"

The singer beamed with joy. And Ma's face? One can well imagine the celestial moments, when like her Master, she gave to this child freedom from fear but fear that one may not achieve that devotion which makes Ma's grace flow and inundate the heart: "But, dear! I want something ……." Ma said.

"Whatever you desire Ma is my *punya* to give. Haven't you given the kind of assurance for which no payment is adequate?"

"I want you to sing another song! That's what I want. Nothing else. You have such wonderful, melodious voice!"

We are intrigued. Does Ma know anything about singing? Of course, she heard her Master's unique rendering of a song. And others. Anything else? Yes, most exhilarating facet: Ma herself sang, sings, thereby, in our hearts. I mean Ma actually sang! Ma was, on that day, talking to Sister Sudhira and others about *Prema-bhakti:* "As one calls on the Master, with sincere faith and devotion, one gets His grace and by that grace *Prema-bhakti,* loving devotion."

Explaining further, the Mother said: "But, mind you, this *Prema-bhakti* is to be cherished, nurtured in utmost privacy, you should note. In absolute solitude *prema* flowers. The gopis of Vraja had this kind of *Bhakti*. Except for their Krishna, they knew nothing. Absolutely nothing. They lived, moved and had their being in, only in, Krishna! But as Nilakantha's song put it: This treasure of Prema must be preserved with the greatest effort!"

And, then, *Ma herself sang!* The blessed ones who heard report: saying all this about *Prema Bhakti*, "the Holy Mother sang the song. In what a sweet voice she sang that day! It is even resounding today in my ears!"

Isn't it echoing even in our ears today? It is. With greater vibrancy. Didn't the mystic-poet assure us: "Heard melodies are sweet! Those unheard are sweeter still!"

But then Ma, let us recall, wanted the beggar-girl – all of us are beggars for love, aren't we? – to sing another song. And the girl did.

Ma, may you be pleased to nurse me as your child!

Let me not grow, leaving behind the beauty of childhood!

A lovely, simple child unaware of honour and dishonour!

Let Me Not Grow

She doesn't know cruelty, nor censure, shame or contempt!

Ma was listening with rapt attention. Instinctively, she exclaimed: "What a soul-stirring song! You are really blessed that you can sing in this beautiful way!"

Happiness lit up the eyes of the singer: "Ma! You like my singing. That makes my heart full! Do you know, Ma, for how many days I was longing to see you! I heard you were here. Wanted to come. Fear overtook me. They may not allow me to…."

Ma promptly said: "None dare do that. None of my children can be denied access to me! Don't you know what my feeling is? I can't contain myself when one draws near me and calls me 'Mother'!

As an epilogue to this let us recall what the Master had to say about Ma's singing. Yogin-Ma tells us: "Ma had a good musical voice. One night she and Lakshmi-Didi were singing in a low tone. It was very resonant and reached the ear of the Master. The next day he said, 'Yesterday, you were singing. That's good, very good.'"

When the Master himself says, "very good," don't we say "Amen!" to that?

Chapter Nineteen

You Are But My Children! What Has Caste to Do With It?

Ma's and the Master's ways are mysterious. Brahmins by birth, they flouted all caste distinctions when they knew the person concerned had transcended them. Or, he or she was ripe enough to be illumined in this regard. But one may ask how do they know? That's a laugh. For, who else knows our past, present and future? Know that our *samskaras*, with a little push, can expedite that awareness which defines a Brahmin as one who has realized Brahman!

A devotee from East Bengal came for Ma's *darshan*. She and her husband came to know about Ma and the Master from that unique disciple: Nag Mahashay. Nag Mahashay had no equal in his devotion: he will even put Anjaneya to flight in that. Nothing else mattered for him except devotion and surrender to the Divine Duo. He always remained in a state of total, incredible dissolution of the ego. He declared: "I am nothing; Sri Ramakrishna is my everything. And I have nothing more to

You Are But My Children! ...

say except with your body, mind and soul take shelter at the holy feet of the Mother and the Master, and it will bring you good."

That was Nag Mahashay and he made this devotee from East Bengal fired with the longing to have *darshan* of Ma. And Ma herself confirmed everything regarding the great devotee's absolute devotion. When she came to know about Nag Mahashay's role in this disciple coming to see her, she herself told the disciple about his extraordinary devotion. She said:

"I wanted to feed him and took a little food. I tried to feed him with this prasada. But he had no outward consciousness. He simply sat touching my feet and saying 'Ma, Ma!' Somehow I managed to make him take some *prasada*. Then he was taken downstairs. And, before he left, his only words were: 'Not I but thou! Not I but thou!'... I knew his surrender was total; *he would do anything for me!*"

Anything! What a simple but stupendous word! Even to contemplate what it implies, brings horripilations all over the body. On the one hand what kind of a Mother, our Ma, must be to inspire such unconditional surrender! On the other what ripeness must be there in the devotee so that the triggering process is electrifying.

Recall Yogin-Ma: at the very first *darshan*, she felt intimate with Ma. And, after some time when Ma left for Kamarpukur, Yogin tells us: "Ma left by boat. As long as it could be seen, I stood gazing at the boat. As soon as the boat was out of sight, I went to the spot in the Nahabat where the Mother used to meditate, and *wept bitterly.*"

The Master heard her weeping and asked her: "Have you been deeply grieved at her departure?"

"Who wouldn't?" One feels like telling the Master: "Who wouldn't be grieved? Is there anything else for those who love you and Ma?"

But then they also weep. Didn't the Master? He did. What about Ma? First, let us listen to the Master's report to Ma after her returned to Dakshineswar: "That girl with big, beautiful eyes loves you dearly. The day you left she *wept bitterly*, sitting in the Nahabat."

Ma nodded. But is she not aware that love only means grief? One can even dare to say, more than the Master, Ma knows the bitterness of love, how heart breaking it is, how shattering it is! To love anyone in general and to love the Master and Ma in particular. Perhaps, it may not be heretical to say: how much inarticulate suffering Ma must have gone through in loving the Master! Inarticulate for the Master had his own divine play. Ma had only the Master! One guesses Ma must have lived only an intense saga of one continuous wailing and weeping for the Master, for her children, for the entire brood, prodigal, profane, indifferent, inane children!

At least in Yogin Ma's case we *know*: She said: "I had come to Vrindavan a few weeks before the demise of the Master. On meeting me at Vrindavan she clasped me to her bosom, *crying in grief*, 'oh, Yogin!' and began to *weep bitterly*."

Weep bitterly seeing Yogin-Ma whom she had met just once. What a wonderful scene! Ma and child together, clasping each other. But Ma also wept quite often. For the Master who assured her, "Here I am, why are you crying!" Ma cries even today… Though few of us realise…

And in the midst of this love can anyone think of distinctions? Didn't the Master say that "Bhaktas are all of one caste!" Ma demonstrated this in her own way. One who inundated Yogin and others with her love will she bother about such tiresome distinctions? After the devotee who came to her inspired by Nag Mahashay was about to leave, Ma made her sit opposite to herself, mixed rice and butter. She then ate three morsels and told the devotee: "Dear! Take this prasada, stretch your palm!"

Ma placed it on her palm pressing it with her hand. And she told her to touch the *prasada* to her head and eat it. The devotee was, obviously, having her own conventional ideas of how an average person belonging to the Brahmin caste observes those conventions. She blurted out, surprised: "Mother! You know I am a Kayastha. But you touched me while taking your food. How will you eat now! Haven't I made you..."

Ma reacted instantly: "You are all my children. Does a mother make caste distinctions among her children! Not only that, between you and me there cannot be any distinction. You are only my children!"

Chapter Twenty
How Innocent Is Our Mother!

The hallmark of innocence is the incurable sense of wonder. Everything that such innocent people see is wonderful, *hear* is wonderful, *talk about* is wonderful. *Ascharya,* wonder, perpetuates and feeds on innocence, guilelessness, even naiveté. These people do not have "the film of familiarity and selfish solicitude" taint or disfigure their lenses of perception. And who can be more innocent than Ma? For her lenses of innocence are not required. For her very eyes are limpid pools of perennial innocence!

Did you note the difference between Ma's and the Master's eyes? Ma's are open; the Master's are half open. And what serenity stares at you in the Mother's eyes! That serene forehead with not a wrinkle, the arched eyebrows and the purity that is imbedded in those eyes! Is it possible for any one – however casually s / he looks – to escape those radiantly subdued eyes which reflect inarticulate, therefore, inescapable, inexpressible wonder and innocence! One feels eternally grateful to Sarah Bull for persuading the Mother to allow her luminous figure to be photographed!

How Innocent Is Our Mother!

Look at the wonder Ma shows towards what we condemn as gadgets. For her there was only wonder and a pointer to the innate creativity of the human consciousness reflected in those things.

It was in May 1914. Golap-Ma, Radhu and a few others were there. It was Ma's visit that excited everyone. Ma's arrival eventually created irrepressible ripples of joy in all. And upstairs, the gramophone was playing. The music flooded the room, one imagines. It must have been an invaluable possession in those days. Perhaps one of those models that one sees in households which we see thanks to filmmakers like Satyajit Ray. And what was Ma's *spandana*, response, to the musical instrument? Immensely pleased, delighted, she articulated her wonder straightaway, spontaneously: "What wonderful machine is this!"

For us coming late in time, alas! machines do not go along with wonder. Too many of them have robbed us of our sense of awe, of wonder at the inexhaustible creations of the human mind! Those who saw Ma's wonder report: Ma was "bubbling with joy like a small girl!"

A small girl, indeed! Ma was above sixty at that time! Age cannot whither nor custom stale her innocence, her joy rooted in a sense of wonder at the inexhaustible ways Nature expresses her creativity. Indeed, Ma, as the disciple rightly said in the hymn, is *"Prakritim Paramam"* who has assumed a human form *"Nararupa Dharam"*! The Paramaprakriti that she is, is it something strange for her to marvel at the ingenuity of her own creation! When she saw the decoration for puja, she exclaimed: "How beautifully has *everything* been arranged!"

Enlarge the context and the words: How beautifully arranged is Ma's creation! No wonder, they say *"She was all praise for everything she saw!"*

For the simple reason that everything reflects her own creative impulse! Her creation is her creativity! Nothing more nothings less.

But she enacts the role she gave herself. And one day Ma tells us: "I had never seen water taps before I came to Calcutta. One day I entered a room where there was a tap. I opened the tap."

Something which we do almost every hour, every day. (Mostly to check whether water is blessing us by its arrival!) But what was Ma's experience?

"Before the water rushed out, there came a hissing sound, like that of a snake out of the tap. I was terror-stricken and ran from the room. I, at once, want to the other ladies of the house and cried, 'There is a snake in that water pipe. It is hissing.'"

What a laughable but deeply moving context where Ma is evidently innocent of what a tap is! Innocent and yet hailed by western women devotees is the Mother of all, the quintessential enlightened womanhood!

And then what happened. The ladies assured Ma: "Nothing to be afraid of, dear. There is no snake in there. The hissing sound comes because the rushing water forces the air in the pipe out!"

All laughed till their sides ached.

Relating this, Ma now also laughed "heartily". "So sweet and innocent a laughter," says Sarayubala and adds, "So guileless our Ma!"

Guileless therefore godly! Innocent therefore illumined. Struck with wonder, therefore wise beyond compare! But, of all these, it is innocence that is the hallmark of Ma. But innocence creates problems. Mother cited an instance: "Once I was deceived by showing affection to Harish!

Chapter Twenty-One

Pipeelikadi Brahma Paryantam!
From the Ant to Brahman, the Ultimate Reality!

The Master's presence (and, of course, Ma's) pervades the entire cosmos. Truths which we read and contemplate in sacred texts come alive in the lives of these two, initially, unanimously anonymous divine duo. One need not invoke Prahalda's assertion that Sri Maha Vishnu is evident, immanent in every object in nature. Since what they create needs to be protected, they do strange things. Strange because we hardly know the range of their operative arena! From the tiny ant to the transcendental Brahman they pervade and penetrate them!

Ma was at Puri Jagannath on a pilgrimage. Why does she go to all these places? Since the Master couldn't go, Ma goes and blesses them – though she stayed rooted in that *Sarvateertha Sanghma Kshetra*, Dakshineswar, the confluence of all holy places.

As soon as Ma alighted at Puri, she wanted to go and see the Lord Jagannath: the Lord of the universe. She knew the special significance that her Lord attached to Puri and Jagannath. Even the mention of Jagannath was ecstatic to him. They were something Ma herself felt. And, therefore, the eagerness to have the *darshan*.

But she had to worship her own Lord and Master every day before she did anything else. The puja, however, in the place she stayed now had necessarily to be in accordance with the facilities available. No altar to be found. Hence, said the Mother, "On the day I reached Puri I quickly finished the worship of the Master, in the morning by placing his picture on a tin containing ghee."

Startling, almost incredible. We, at a later date, used to the opulence of the altars and the grandeur of the temples that Thakur resides in, find it incredible that he rested in a picture kept, of all things, on a tin! And that too containing ghee. "Wherever you keep me, I shall live there!" said the Master to his favourite *chela*: Swamiji. Will he do less in the case of his own consort who came to be the counterpart of Shakti to his Shiva? "It hardly matters. Whether you keep me on an altar in the temple or on a tin in a room in a *dharamshala*, I shall abide there!" he would have declared.

After the worship was over, Ma locked the room and went to the temple and saw the Lord of the Universe in, as it were, his own habitat! The grandeur and the holiness must have been overpowering. And certainly the Master must have appeared in that image which is his own vibrant form in another context and at another time. We see the images now and feel immeasurably blessed: for we see images which those divine eyes *saw* and therefore, if one is lucky, *see* the images as not icons but as living flames of timeless reality blazing forth their splendour for uplifting the consciousness of the devout, the destitute and the despised!

Ma returned to the room, the joy of the *darshan* writ large on her radiant face. She opened the room, entered and perhaps wanted to do *pranams* to *her* Lord. Then she noted the odd thing. She called out to her companions and said: "Do you see what had happened? Isn't it strange?"

"What's strange, Mother? We don't see anything that is so, as you say, strange! Nothing is missing. The door is locked. You yourself opened it!" one of the devotees said.

"Observe carefully. Didn't I place Thakur's picture on this tin containing ghee?"

"Yes, you did. We did pranams, too."

"See now. It's at the foot of the tin. How did it come there? Who moved it? And why?"

Ma was obviously baffled. The companions saw it: Yes, the picture was at the foot of the tin. How did it happen? And it was not tilted or lying upside down if something or someone moved it. You can't expect the picture to move on its own…

But that's exactly what happened. The mystery now became a revelatory text! Ma relentlessly pursued her quest. How did the picture move? When everything else in the room remained in its place. Except the Master, everything else remained *status quo*.

Finally, Ma pierced to the root of the mystery. And with eagerness and relief told the companions: "I found out the reason at last. Don't you see those red ants, rather big ants which gathered on the tin? Ghee tin! And ants are bound to come!"

"That's true, Ma! At last you found out the reason…," said one of the companions.

The words trailed off. But ants don't move picture, do they? Inconceivable, to say the least. That reason ruled out. We are left with an enigma. And how disarmingly but breathtakingly – for us - Ma reveals the truth! She said: *"It's a tin full of ghee, since they had approached the picture of the Master also, he had come down and settled himself below!"*

"Came down!" oh my God! Don't we say to ourselves? We long to believe it; a few blessed souls have *natural faith* which makes it possible for them to believe any and everything. On behalf of the devotees' occupying the twilight zone of faith and skepticism, a disciple asked: "Does the Master really live in the picture?"

Really live – that is the question. Our reality is not real enough to contain or confine the Real. 'The Real' that all scriptures invoke as the goal to reach from the unreal. We are caught in between. Even when the Master assured Ma and thereby us after – for want of words, we say – his passing away. "What are you doing? I *have not gone away. I have only passed from one room to another."*

We can in this context phrase it: he passed from that Cosmic Form into the *form that is written with light*. For, doesn't a photograph mean "writing with light" and didn't Ma admire the enormous intelligence behind this discovery? Ma's answer was therefore decisive: "Of course, he does. The body and the shadow are the same. And what is his picture but a shadow!"

Look at the word: "Picture". Ma doesn't say a "photo". Any picture. If the proof is indeed looked at, to take one example, the picture drawn by Frank Dvorak! Surely, the Master entered it! But then we get a lingering doubt. We can't help it. Ma knew this and told us that it is due to the very intelligence that we pride ourselves about:

The intelligence of a man is very precarious. It is like the thread of a screw. If one thread is loosened, then he goes crazy. Or he becomes entangled in the trap of Mahamaya and thinks himself to be very intelligent.

This is the origin of doubt. In the present context it gets phrased thus: "It's all right Ma. It is *your* picture. Does *he live in all the pictures?*"

Ma was forthright: "Yes. If you pray to him constantly before his picture then he manifests himself through that picture. The place where the picture is kept becomes a shrine!"

If you pray: that is the key that clarifies. What has happened is not magic or miracle. It is not the result of any *siddhi*. All miracles are, as Sri Ram says, encounters between our love and God's love. When they coalesce the miracle of love envelops one and enlightens. Enlightens us about the fact: as Ma puts it: "Certainly you will have doubts. There will be questions and faith will return again. *That is how faith is established.*"

Whether we believe it or not, have faith or not, the incontestable truth is: Ma and the Master pervade the cosmos from the *pipeelika* to Brahman!

Chapter Twenty-Two
Call on the Mother Alone!

Ma's *lilas,* pastimes, are unending. And if there is a tie between Ma and the Master, it is generally Ma who triumphs and the Master has to yield! What a couple they are! Outwitting each other in everything but also complementing each other. No wonder Ma Sarada is *Ramakrishna Gathaprana!*

Vaikuntha was one of those blessed ones whom Ma favoured, on her own, with *Mantra diksha.* And, in some contexts, she specifically directed him to do according to her instructions. Perhaps, Vaikuntha didn't realize fully the significance of what Ma says and does.

"Vaikuntha," the Mother told him one day. "Go and visit the temple of Raghuvira and offer some money in the temple. If you don't have money, I shall give you some."

Vaikuntha, accordingly, went to the temple and came back: "Ma! As you suggested. I have gone to the temple!"

Call on the Mother Alone!

So saying he made pranams to the Mother. The Mother was obviously pleased. But after a few minutes Ma suddenly said!

"Vaikuntha, take my name!" It came abruptly. There was no context for Ma to say such a thing. Vaikuntha didn't ask for any such thing but unexpectedly Ma asked him to take *her* name. Perhaps, Vaikuntha was bewildered. Much more of a puzzle waited for him. After an instant, Ma said: "Vaikuntha! Call on the Master. Calling on the Master will alone serve everything."

Along with Vaikuntha, we are also puzzled. Ma says, "Take my name" and the next moment exhorts Vaikuntha to call on the Master and that *alone* will serve everything. Is Ma playing with us, intentionally, to confuse us? That cannot be. For Ma will never confuse her children.

Lakshmi-didi, present there when Ma made the two statements, realised that the context and the statement have profound significance. There is in it more than what meets the eye. But she had to be sure about that. So she asked Ma somewhat annoyed: "Ma! This is the limit! How can you say two things at the same time? Isn't it most confusing to your children?"

Ma appeared taken aback: "What is confusing in what I said? I don't find any!"

"You don't find any confusion? One moment you told Vaikuntha 'call on me' and in the next, you are saying 'call on the Master!' what do we make out of this?"

Ma, to put a lid on the confusion as it were, again said: "Everything is achieved when one calls on the Master!"

Perhaps, the significance was not fully understood by Lakshmi-didi. She reiterated: "Ma! Why do you confuse your children in this way? Is it proper?"

Is it confusion? You simply change the spelling; remove "con", you are left with "fusion". Ma and the Master are not separate, separable beings. They are the two faces of the same coin! Didn't the Mother say at one point: "Think of me and the Master as one!" Not only that when someone asked, "What should I think of you?" She made an extremely revealing statement: *"Think of me as Radha!"* And, by implication, the Master is Krishna. Is there any difference between them? How can one forget that moment of cosmic oneness when as a culmination of Shodasi worship, both Ma and the Master became and ever since remain one! They represent the Upanishadic truth of the *Poornam;* wholeness with functional differentiation. Functional not intrinsic or inherent.

But Ma rarely makes such statements. *That* is the uniqueness. If the Master himself rarely makes full affirmations, Ma is rarer. She is the classic instance of *apaurushey satya rupa:* the truth of the impersonal which, as Thakur said, thanks to the love and devotion of a bhakta gets solidified into a concrete form. Perhaps, my own case is typical: I was initiated during the Mother's centenary celebrations in 1953, but my mantra had Thakur as the *Ishta Daiva.* Both Ma and Master came to bless this errant, prodigal child! However, Ma never volunteers affirmations that point to such enormous truths.

Lakshmi-didi, in a flash, intuited the significance. She was no longer confused or bewildered. She hit the bull's eye: "Vaikuntha! You are so fortunate! For the first time we heard Ma say 'call on Me!' Get the point.

Call on the Mother Alone!

Don't miss it. Or, take it as a play. Ma is telling the Truth. *You call on the Mother alone.* How much of *punya* you must have done that you get the advice, the instruction from Ma herself! *Call on the Mother alone!*"

And Lakshmi-didi did something else. She turned towards Ma and asked: "Ma! Isn't this the right thing? What I said is true? Isn't it?"

Profound silence pervaded the Mother. And in such silence – where baffled words come back – are born perceptions which transform consciousness, making it take a quantum leap into – where else – the lap of our lovely Ma!

But, then, don't miss "Vaikuntha". They say, it means the space where the all-bewitching Mahamaya doesn't function to trap us!

One also recalls Tanmayananda's revelation. He tells us an amazing parallel to what Vaikuntha experienced: "I worshipped Ma with flowers and bilwa leaf. I prostrated to her and then put her holy feet on my head. Ma said: "Dear! One's feet should not be kept on the head. Thakur is there."

The devotee was frank and forthright: "Ma! I haven't seen Thakur. But now I'm seeing my Thakur before me!"

Ma replied: "No, dear! The Lord is there, seated in the thousand-petaled lotus."

Pat came the million-dollar question, if you can put it that way: "If Thakur is God, Bhagawan, who are you, Ma?"

"Who am I? I am also a Goddess!"

The narrator says, "I felt a thrill all over my body!" Don't we all feel the same?

Chapter Twenty-Three
A Porter But a Chosen One!

Mysterious are Ma's ways in pulling the potential one to her fold! It could even be what most people dismiss as a mere dream. Whatever it is, where there is *Vyakulatha*, intense longing, there is Ma's *Vyaktikavana*, her manifest form.

Gauri-Ma's tale tells the truth of this.

Ma was at the Vishnupur railway station, expecting her train. By the way, whenever we hear of the vehicles Ma used for traveling we feel like saying what Ramachandra Dutta told devotees: "Everything that Thakur touched *is* sacred. Go and touch those horses and that carriage! They have carried Thakur many times!" One feels like saying, "Go and touch that bullock cart and those bullocks! They carried Ma! Imagine, Ma carries the weight of the cosmos and that cart and those cattle carried her weight! Isn't it intriguing?" Similarly, go and stand on the platform of Vishnupur railway station and take some dust off it! Ma waited there for her train! And look for the porter!

Ma must be enjoying the spectacle. From the bullock cart to the train! Quite a transition!

Suddenly, someone was seen rushing to Ma. A porter, judged by his dress. He saw her from a distance and ran. The travelers must have wondered: What has happened to him? The train is not sighted, yet. No, he was not running to catch a traveler and snatch the weight of his or her luggage! He was running to lay down the burden, the anguish of his longing at the feet of his Ma! And Ma wasn't surprised, presumably. She knew. The man said, they say, in Hindi: "You are my Mother Janaki! I was searching for you all these days. And thought I will not have the good fortune of seeing you. Where were you, Ma, for so long?"

Even as he spoke, the voice choked and tears swept his whole being. He wept and wept. How blessed is he to weep and shed tears for Ma! Didn't Thakur say: "People shed jug full of tears, for enjoyment, for children etc, who will shed tears for God?" Here is one who has kept– preciously – those tears for shedding now! Ma was neither embarrassed nor taken aback. She *knew*. She consoled him: "Dear! Don't weep! Your very tears have brought you to me."

The porter was overjoyed. At last his chosen ideal was before him in flesh and blood! It is like Sudama seeing Sri Krishna and getting overwhelmed by his friend's all-encompassing love!

Ma asked him: "Can you bring a flower? Will one be available? Now?"

Her *samkalpa* materializes whatever it wants. No wonder and in no time, the porter brought a flower and placed it at her lotus feet. *"Patram, Pushpam, Phalam, Toyam"* says the Lord in the *Gita*. Bring me "a leaf, a flower, a fruit or a drop of water!" The porter brought a flower and for water what can be better and more precious than tears?

Ma initiated him. Imagine: even the most devoted aspirant fails to get the Mother's *mantra diksha*. Here is one who got just like that gentle dew that falls unseen but here it fell seen, not unseen! The porter's cup was full. He can now bear any weight on his head – for it is illusion to think that we bear the weight. Does anyone carry a load on his head after getting into the train? You place it on the floor and relax. Place all burdens at her feet and relax. (It looks so simple but alas! How stupendous surrender is!)

Gauri-Ma wondered: "How could this man *recognise* Ma? And hold Mother as Janaki, Sri Ram's consort? Otherwise, one can't explain his search. Perhaps, he had a dream…"

Does it matter? The porter has been pulled into the vast perennial pool of Ma's pure love. *Bas!*

Chapter Twenty-Four
Called Compassionate: But No Trace of It!

Once Thakur advised that if you feel a negative emotion, direct it to God. Then it becomes positive. Feel angry? Direct it to God: "What! I have prayed and wept so long. How dare you don't appear?"

Ma sat for puja but couldn't go on. A song coming from below drew her attention:

You are called compassionate, but no trace of compassion in you!

You have severed the heads of others,

Put on as a garland of heads on your neck

How much I call you as Mother! Mother!

Though you hear, pretend as if you did not hear

Even getting hit, Nara calls you as Durga!

The song matched the mood and voice of the singer. There was anger subdued, though. There was audible frustration, a helplessness that was heart-rending. Otherwise, will anyone dare to sing a song ridiculing the

Mother, taunting her in fact? Or, will the singing reach Ma, in the first place?

Who is this seeker who dared to disturb Ma at puja? A strange phenomenon. But who can gauge the irrepressible urge that tugs at the heart that wrenches one from one's moorings and sets up a wailing which articulated through as songs which reflects comparable agony?

But why such desperation? Vasantha Sarkar took *diksha* from Ma and his wife, too, wanted it. But Ma said: "There are many *sadhus* at Belur Math. You go there and take initiation. It isn't possible for me, child."

The lady was aghast. She didn't expect such a turn of events. She appealed to Ma: "With great difficulty I came, Ma. I had even gone into debt. To get refuge at your lotus feet. If I am denied that, I can't think of even going home. And Ma, about my *diksha*. I will not take it from any other!"

The Mother was a bit annoyed: "You know you are very stubborn! You won't even listen to what I said. And perhaps I have to blame Thakur, too. He left all these things to me and I can't bear the burden of these responsibilities!"

Mrs Sarkar was totally upset. And the prospect of not getting *diksha* from Ma filled her with such agony that she spontaneously burst into song! The pathos of which moved Ma so deeply that she couldn't even do puja. She realised Mrs Sarkar's great longing for diksha and that from herself alone! Above all, she knew that what appeared as the lady's stubbornness and helpless anger in fact reflected her strong conviction, her *sraddha*. And can Ma refuse? She came down from the puja and called her and said laughing: "You are mad! You know that? But you have quite a few signs of a good seeker."

Called Compassionate: But No Trace of It!

The lady interrupted eagerly: "So you will bless me with *diksha*, won't you, Ma?"

Mother said: "I liked your signing. Do sing another song – for me. Won't you?"

The lady sang again, pouring her heart and soul into the song. Singing over, Ma told her: "Child! Your singing is so sweet that I couldn't even do puja. I shall do my puja now – allow me! You take some rest."

Needless to say, Ma fixed a date for her initiation. The compassionate Ma appears cruel only to be kind. And her *delays* are not *denials*. Didn't she herself declare, "If one is without kindness, how can one be called a human being? And the purpose of one's life is fulfilled only when one is able to give joy to another." If the devotee's singing gave Ma *bhajanananda*, Ma gave her something much, much more enduring. *Dikshananda!*

But, the question is: why did Ma refuse to give *diksha* in the first instance! And gave it later. Aurpananda raised this question: "You willingly give Mantra to people, Ma. Don't you? Then why do you seem unwilling in this case?"

Ma promptly said: "Out of compassion. They don't leave me alone. Not just that: they start weeping profusely. And that makes my heart melt."

Explaining further Ma added: "It is only compassion for them that makes me yield and give *diksha;* giving diksha is not a simple thing. I have to accept the sins of all those to whom I give initiation. And you know what I say to myself? 'This body is certain to go one day or the other. Let my children be benefited.'"

Chapter Twenty-Five
No Use Repairing It. It Reminds Me of Yogin!

Unfathomable are Ma's actions and their implied significances. Often it is not so much her imperceptible but infinite splendour that catches us as her intensely human, indeed simple, acts. Why she does such things is not a mystery. Everything about her lives, moves and has its being in love. Of varied hues is this love, a many-splendoured rainbow. Her love is irresistible: You are helpless. It inundates you, intoxicates you. And recovering from that intoxication is only to wonder: "Is such love possible? The tiniest gesture on your part is enough for Ma to feel immeasurably happy and *loyal t*o your gesture! Is it credible?" That's her magic...

Yogin-Ma had prepared a mattress for Ma. With what dedication Yogin served Ma! Her sole concern was to keep her in comfort, free from all troubles which, alas, surrounded her! At least let her have a mattress for some comfort, thought Yogin and made one. Ma used it with joy. Indeed, Ma had this "habit" of treasuring everything that anyone gave – however trivial – out of respect and affection for the person who gave it.

Perhaps, in her cosmos everything is imbued with Love and that makes it priceless. Ma declared once: "Is the value of a thing to be gauged by its price? It is the love and affection with which a thing is offered that really counts."

But then one gets things which wear out. What do we do? The mattress became worn out, tattered. She called a devotee, Vibhuti Babu. "Vibhuti! You know Yogin gave this mattress to me. As you can see, it is worn out. Can you take out the old cotton and put it inside a new cover?"

Vibhuti Babu felt privileged to do this for Ma: "Certainly Ma. I will buy a new cover and get the cotton stuffed into that as you desire!"

And he left, saying that he will take it later and arrange for whatever is to be done in this regard. Ma looked at the mattress again and felt a shock: "What am I doing? Giving a new shape to something dear Yogin gave me! Why should I do this kind of thing? Perhaps, I never realised: the mattress in a new form loses its very identity! A new one is not and cannot be the one that Yogin gave me. It should be kept as a priceless treasure of her love and not something to be recycled for reuse!"

Vibhuti came to collect it and Ma said: "No, Vibhuti. I have changed my mind. There is no need for changing the cover. It is a token of Yogin's love. And whenever I see it I remember Yogin! Isn't that more valuable than continuing to value is for its use?"

Things most valuable have quite often no use. To value it for continuing use is to be, in essence, what Thakur called "the rice and plantain-bundling priest." We know, in our consumerist milieu, we have reduced all values to prices and implied that priceless things are valueless things. Ma prizes compassion and love; we prize possession and use.

Like in Kalidas's *Sakuntalam*. You can buy a new golden ring worthy of an emperor. But you require only that ring which symbolised love and love alone and will reveal the secret of their *Gandharva Vivaha*. Not the ring *per se* but what it radiated!

Ma's method is not to pontificate as I am doing but to show. And another context came, this time involving a sovereign.

Phani Bhushan (later Bhavesananda) had been to the Great War (obviously the first one) and brought a Turkish sovereign. He caught hold of a devotee and requested him to give it to Ma. The devotee went to Ma: "Ma! You know Phani Bhushan! He had gone to the war and came back. He brought a Turkish sovereign with him and wanted me to give it to you!"

Don't imagine that Ma does not know about war and related things. When the war situation was reported to her she made a very insightful remark about the freedom of the country. Similarly, a disciple told Ma: "Ma! Many young men are being jailed by the government now. What will be the outcome of all this?"

Ma straight away said: "It's improper. No doubt about it. However, a solution will soon be found. You will not have to wait for long. It will certainly bring good."

To resume: the sovereign was in Ma's hands. Perhaps, she thought for a minute. We do not know. But we do know her response: "What value and worth this sovereign has? However, I shall keep it. As a remembrance of the person who has sent it. With what intense feeling he must have sent it!"

No Use Repairing It. It Reminds Me of Yogin!

What a parallel to the classic equation of the Master! *Taka mati, mati taka!* Money is mud, mud is money! But with a difference. Ma found the gold as a symbol of the sender's devotion. In other words, Ma and the Master do not despise money. It has use including the value of a symbol. Beyond that they become impediments. Indicating covetousness, greed. And Ma valued the feelings of the sovereign sender so that she kept it carefully. After she passed away, they found it wrapped securely in a paper in a box! Like us, her children, wrapped in the raiment of her invaluable love.

With what ingenuity and finesse, Ma put to use things which have no intrinsic value for her. The Master always said that if you put a zero before it will not enhance its value. But place if after one, it enhances and make one acquire the value of ten. Similar is the case with things.

Nivedita once gave Ma a German silver casket. God or silver, boxes are only functional. And Ma accepted it and put the most precious memento in that: the Master's hairs! A box for the Master's hair it was also a *pratybhijna,* a token of recognition. Ma declared: "When I do puja, the sight of the casket flashes the memory of Nivedita in my mind!"

One can call such incidents where memory is ignited *Ma Sarada's Spanda Karikas,* incidents of vibrant memories where the object concerned is a catalytic agent. Or if one prefers the idiom of management they constitute communication by trigger. The object's apparent value is extremely disproportionate to the real, that is, its intrinsic value.

Let us contemplate another revealing *spanda katha:* Ma was going from Jayarambati to Calcutta. There was some luggage and Ma was searching for something. A devotee noticed this and asked Ma: "What are you searching for Ma? Can I help you?"

"Yes. Where did you keep that Bala-Posh (cotton wrapper)? I can't find it anywhere."

In fact, that devotee managed to keep all things in an orderly, systematic way. He was, in effect, the caretaker. But he also couldn't find the wrapper Ma wanted. Crestfallen, he told Ma: "Mother! You must forgive me. I don't recall where I kept it. It saddens me. How disorganised I am in keeping things in a tidy manner."

Ma too felt very sad. It was inexplicable.

Then Ma said: "Search for it again! Perhaps, it is tucked away somewhere and you forgot that you kept it there."

That was exactly what had happened. After a vigorous search, it was found in a place they had hardly suspected it would be. There was visible happiness on Ma's face. The 'manager' was intrigued. Why was Ma so particular? It was so inexplicable. One could easily replace the thing with a new one. It wasn't very expensive. Ma knew that kind of thinking. She said with visible delight and joy: "You may think of what worth is that Bala-posh? Not much, yes. But it was a gift from Balaram Babu's mother! That's why I felt such anxiety."

Ma is right, we all confuse value and price. And assume that everything has a price and is available for a price. For instance, buy an expensive bed, a scandalously costly dinner, and a palatial home. An expensive, comfortable bed may not ensure sleep. And if you do sleep, any bed is as good as another. Similarly, delicious food is delicious only when you have hunger. And, we all know, palatial houses, quite often, are poor homes!

No Use Repairing It. It Reminds Me of Yogin!

Finally, a deeply moving moment of love that cares for nothing except the sanctity and holiness which that love causes. Surendranath Sircar was the lucky one.

Sircar made what looks like a strange request to Ma: "Ma! I want to ask you for something. Shall I?"

"Dear! Why do you hesitate? After all, I am your Mother. Am I not!"

"That is why I want to ask. Ma! Everything associated with you is holy, Ma. And one should be really fortunate to posses any such thing. Please give me one of the saris you wore, Ma!"

Ma smiled. It was, perhaps, to be expected. Only the day before Sircar brought some saris for Mother and insisted: "Ma! Please accept these saris. And you must wear them yourself. Don't distribute them to others as, they say, you do!"

This was the precedent. Ma gladly gave a sari to Sircar but told him: "Son! It is quite dirty, unclean. Please wash it."

"No, Mother! I want to preserve it exactly in the condition in which you have gifted it to me. I don't want to send it to a laundry!"

Ma knew the profound devotion he had. In the face of devotion, do the categories of clean, unclean function? And is total devotion anything more than *param prem*, supreme love?

Chapter Twenty-Six
If You Want Peace...

Ma was already severely ill. She sent away Radhu, the binding link to the world of life and death and all those that they involve. Devotees guessed. Ma was preparing for *Mahasamdhi*.

Can one contemplate the passing of Ma? Without breaking one's heart? For us who come late, chronologically, it is an agonizing spectacle. "Oh Ma, you submit to your own rules. All that are born must pass!" – we feel like saying.

But then Ma never leaves us. We may leave her. That is possible, almost predictable. But she doesn't. Even then we wonder. And one devotee articulated the predicament for all of us: "Mother! What will happen to us?"

Ma called the mother of Annapurna who asked the question near. With a feeble voice Ma said: "You have had *darshan* of Thakur. Then why do you fear? I will tell you one thing – if you want peace, do not find fault with others. See your own faults. Learn to make the whole world your own. Nobody is a stranger, my dear. The whole world belongs to you."

"If you want peace". Note the condition "if". Do we want? Then, wanting it is to follow Ma's (and the Master's) footsteps. Follow their path of *Parama prema*. That is their miracle of love.

Chapter Twenty-Seven
Not Just *Darshan* But Initiation Too

The sanyasins protested vehemently: "You should not have done this, Mother. It is certainly against all ethics. We expected you to turn the fellow out. He had no business to butt in!"

Of course, they were right in their own way. How can an immoral character, steeped in vice, sunk in sin, expect the Holy Mother to see him? The consort of Sri Ramakrishna, Sarada Ma—how can one admit such a person to her presence? Compassion is the very essence of Ma. But they felt even the all-encompassing compassion has limits.

It all started when Mother heard that her sanyasin children had turned away an allegedly depraved man from seeing her. "We turned him away: we didn't even allow him to come anywhere near the Udbodhan," they told Mother. They knew that Mother had an orthodox background and was the purest of the pure. An incredibly immaculate Mother, she was. And they felt that Mother would be pleased by their concern and care to protect her from all and sundry. That was their *dharma*.

But they didn't reckon with the firmness that underlay Mother's gentle nature. Especially in the context of offering consolation and solace to the destitute, the decadent and the degraded. Did not her Lord tell her that he was leaving her behind to complete and continue the work for which they both took human form and came together? The inseparable Shiva and Shakti.

No wonder she instantly said: "Bring the man here! I want him to see me! Didn't I tell you that no one—I repeat, *no one* is a stranger to me! So go after him quickly and bring him in!"

They did. They could not ignore her words. The man came hesitantly but joy suffusing his face. Even disbelief that such a fortune should befall him. He dare not hope to enter that holy place sanctified by so many saintly men and women. He approached Mother with, one can imagine, downcast eyes. Not daring to look at her face: the face that all the goddesses were invoked in and adorned by Ramakrishna, the Great Master, himself.

Mother had other blessings than mere *darshan*. She said to the hapless man: "Have a wash. Come into the puja room. I shall give you a *mantra*. Do japa regularly and see what a change it will bring in your life!"

That's when the disciples protested. And what did Mother of all say? *"You have nothing to interfere with in this matter. I can do as I wish."*

Perhaps, in retrospect, one would simply say: yes, they come for the prodigal children more than the upright (uptight?) ones. Yes, Mother's wish is instant will. *Iccha* becomes *kriya shakti*. How lucky was the one who got the mantra!

Girish Chandra Ghosh and Binodini would certainly endorse, if not envy, the inestimable luck of the man.

Chapter Twenty-Eight

No Complaints, Please! (And Certainly No Lectures on Vedanta!)

The Mother and Master were passing through Kamarpukur. The village that is now on the landscape of spiritual world. Master was enjoying every sight and sound: the place filled with memories of an ecstatic childhood. Bliss was it, to be alive and be a child in that village! (An Eternal Child, in this case). He was pointing out familiar landmarks to his *sahadharmini*, his—as he himself called—*Shakti*. "See that is the grove where we used to sit and regale ourselves with stories of all kinds. What a joy it was then! Pack some *muri* into a tiny basket and sling it across our shoulder and roam at will!"

Mother too was enjoying his delight. "Yes; simple things are his staple diet of spirituality. Everything and anything is a marvel to him, the birds in the sky, the rushing streams, the stillness of water in a tank, the fish floating in them, the sunrise, the sunset, the stars in the sky! Everything plunges him into *samadhi*!" Mother was thinking, looking at his face, radiant with the sheer texture of whatever he was experiencing!

No Complaints, Please!

Suddenly, Thakur shouted, "Hey you, Hriday! Come over here. What is happening to this house?" They entered his old house. Things were not right. The kitchen, specially, was rapidly decomposing itself. Thakur was upset, visibly and ticked off Hriday: "You are supposed to look after the house here—periodically at least. Obviously you don't do anything of that nature. Isn't it neglect and carelessness which, you know, I cannot tolerate? Hire someone and get the house back to its spick and span appearance!"

Ma was watching all this quietly and she knew that Hriday did not deserve that kind of reprimand that he was getting now. How faithfully and faultlessly he had served Him! And for so many years. Indeed, during the *sadhana* period it was he who kept the Master's physical frame alive. Even to the point of thrusting some food down his throat. The dressing he was getting now was unfair.

Ma turned to Master and in a gentle but firm tone (which did not mince matters) exclaimed: "How frequently do you come to your village? Not regularly, I suppose. You come now and then, today the only thing you do, first thing in the morning, is scold poor Hriday! You know what and how much he did for you!"

Thakur obviously was taken aback. Mother rarely spoke in a raised voice. Gentle in words, modest in her behavior and gestures, rarely did she talk as she was doing now. Mother made an assertion which created, one imagines, a ripple of disquiet in Master's mind: "You come like lightning to this place and leave as quickly. *You are very selfish*!" added Mother.

Thakur selfish? Unthinkable, indeed, incredible. Master got an opening to reply, "Yes," he conceded, "I *am* selfish, but it is not love of the little self but of the Universal Self." And Mother said, recalling the incident, "Thakur stood there and gave me a lecture on Vedanta, for half an hour at least!"

No complaints, please, she says and what she gets is a lecture on Vedanta. Naturally, Mother was astonished, they say, "mildly."

The divine couple has their own wavelength, their idiosyncratic ways of responding to situations. But complaints galore, *we* make. And when advice is given, don't we sidetrack the issue and talk about other things, chief of which is defending ourselves? The Mother is simple: no complaints and conceding. Only, concern with what is to be done. No lecture in reply, only letting go other things and letting in what is to be done and doing it. We suppose Hriday did what had to be done—as the Master wanted.

Chapter Twenty-Nine
The Divine Mother Who Fans and Feeds

A teacher he was by profession. Quite young, dedicated to his job and also an ardent devotee of Ma. He longed to have her *darshan* frequently. But, alas, he lived some twenty-five miles away from Ma's place. So, if he had to see his beloved Ma he could do that only on a holiday. And he did get a holiday one day.

Perhaps, he couldn't afford any carriage or even a bullock cart. But his intense desire to have the Mother's *darshan* gave him wings, so to say! He took to the road, walked all the twenty-five miles at a stretch with the Mother's radiant face beckoning him all the way. He covered the distance in no time and arrived at Mother's place.

Mother was delighted to see her son. But she knew that walking that long stretch was not a joke. She saw him sweating—almost panting. The long stretch of walk had sapped all his energy. Mother asked him: "Why did you walk all the way, my child? See how your whole body is covered with dust! And how breathless you are from the long walk! Come, sit here on this mat!"

He fell at her feet and touched it with that reverence which only ardent faith and love generate. But Mother was doing something else. She pulled an old-fashioned palm-leaf fan from the thatched roof, made the young teacher sit on the mat and started fanning him! She whom Thakur himself had worshipped on that remarkable day—the Shodasi—as the Divine Mother herself, as her incarnate human form, fanning a school teacher!

"Oh, Mother! Please don't embarrass me! It is the very height of sinful irreverence for me to accept your service. You are the One, the Divine Mother, who should receive our service and not be served by you!"

Ma smiled, remaining silent and continued fanning the fortunate *adyapak*. Perhaps, she remembered the Master, her Lord's words: "You are the same Mother who is my Mother, and the Divine Mother Kali herself!" Yes, she is the Mother of all, the Mother who germinated all the Mothers, the Root Mother, with many roles she has to play in the divine drama, the *lila* that her Lord and Master (and the Lord of all) brings into being.

Don't imagine fanning is a trivial thing. It is not a fan which with the press of a switch fills the space with air. It is a fan you have to rotate continuously with the hand. And Ma did it for half an hour! The Mother whose boundless love cools and fans the body and mind filled with the fever of worldliness—or woman and gold—fanning her fond child! Nothing can be more fascinating!

"Are you feeling better now? OK, then go and have a wash. I shall prepare a meal for you . . . . I don't know when you started for this place. Perhaps, you haven't even had some *muri* in the morning before you started . . . . But I *know* you are hungry!"

Ma went into the kitchen and prepared not just a Spartan lunch but a heavy meal. She cooked it herself: the Annapurna who feeds every child, coming straight from the pages of the Puranas and preparing food for her children. The Ever Fullness Incarnate—*Sadapurne*—the Infinite Unfathomable Abundance, abiding there in those thatched huts anonymously and cooking, washing, cleaning, nursing, nourishing her children.

"Come and eat and don't feel shy. Don't you know my child Narendra said that to the hungry God comes in the form of delicious food?"

The schoolteacher was not a teacher for nothing. He could guess: "Mother, I don't know all that. It is beyond me. I know that you are my Mother! Or, rather, you are all the Gods and Goddesses together."

Mother smiled. "Then I will have to, like Mother Kali, stick out my tongue and stand on a pedestal," she said.

"You don't have to, Mother. This time, it is a baffling, anonymous avatar," the teacher started saying.

Ma intervened firmly, "*Bas*, don't bother about all those things. I am your Ma. Know that and that's enough. And now eat . . . ."

The teacher enjoyed his food as he perhaps never did before. Food? No, prasada from the Perennial Divine Feminine, the Primordial Shakti that rules the world and rocks it into sleep when the time comes.

The inmates were watching everything: amazed, baffled; how could the Mother take so much trouble? She, the counterpart of the great Paramahamsa, doing all this? They didn't realise that this was not all.

The schoolteacher did pranams to Mother and was about to leave. "Come, I shall see you off," she said.

"No, Mother I won't allow you to do that. I shall go, no problem," he firmly declared. Mother meant what she said. She was already on the road.

The teacher had no option. He meekly followed her. But tears welled up in his eyes, "Is such concern and compassion conceivable? Will anyone believe it?" By this time, they were already on the edge of the fields. Mother bade him goodbye. He did pranams and set off, as if walking on air.

But did he know that Ma stood rooted there for nearly an hour, looking at him with those eyes, perennial pools of infinite compassion—until he was out of sight? (But not out of her heart, never!)

Chapter Thirty
Fault Finders All: But Let Me Be an Exception!

Mother is *Prakriti*, the *moola prakriti* of the cosmos. And in *prakriti*, Nature, there is nothing that is a *vikriti*, or unnatural aberrations. Hierarchies, high and low, superior, inferior are functional. But in the world of names and forms one has varied dimensions. And even incarnations register authentic emotions that evoke grief, the infinite sorrow that stems from inability to see the apparent defects.

The shouting was almost deafening. Golap-Ma was at it: "You are always careless! How many times have I told you! To be careful. You never listen." "Maji! I am always careful . . . only this time, a little milk overflowed from the pot . . ." the maidservant didn't even finish. Golap-Ma cut her short, "You think it is little milk! Half a pot is empty. And you call it little! The cheek!" The maidservant looked obviously upset. She was being ticked off for a negligible incident.

Mother was watching the whole thing with interest. And, it seemed with suppressed amusement. She knew Golap was a stickler for discipline.

And she never tolerated inefficiency, sloppiness of any kind. She had no use for excuses and explanations. She looked for meticulous doing of things. Nothing more, nothing less. How sad! Mother thought. She recalled what she did in the morning, almost everyday.

It was the temple of Radharaman, while she was in Vrindavan. She prayed fervently: "O Lord! Remove from me the tendency, the habit of finding fault with others!" She used to add, "There are spots on the moon, even the moon! But let me be spotless!"

What a strange spectacle! Can anyone believe the Divine Mother doing such a thing! Yes, she can. To give us the model of life that is based not on faultfinding but on assuring that in Mother's creation evil, faults, etc, are dramatic requirements of the Cosmic play. And in the ultimate analysis, isn't it fascinating that the Ma who is praying in this context is exactly the Divine Mother to whom we pray—to remove our blind spots?

Mother is perfect in designing and drawing a scene to its most dramatic close. As if not knowing the reason for Golap-Ma's anger, she asked, "What is the provocation, Golap, for this anger? Did the servant do anything terrible?" Golap-Ma was still nursing her anger, and flared up at Mother: "Why are you asking? Is there any point in telling you the reason?" "Why not? I can think of what is to be done," said Mother. "You thinking of what is to be done? You who *cannot* see the defects of others!" Golap-ma retorted.

Mother's face glowed with a strange light. As if she was like a child guessing a secret well-hidden from all. She said with conviction and candor: "Well, Golap, people who see the faults of others are dime a

Fault Finders All: But Let Me Be an Exception!

dozen. It is congenital! The world will not stop ticking if I am differently made. Yes, they are *my* children. How can a mother find blemishes in her beautiful children? That is absurd. So let me be an exception to the rule."

Chapter Thirty-One
Touch Me, That's Enough

Mother, unlike Father, rarely gave glimpses of the enormous Reality she embodied. Like the veil with which she covered her luminous face, she concealed her identity. But in moments where only such an epiphany could set things right, she didn't hesitate. But such a revelation arose from multiple needs.

It was nine o' clock in the night. Generally, visitors are rare at that hour. Not many dared to see Ma at odd hours. Even her beloved children, the Master's direct disciples, hesitated, if at all they decided to have her *darshan* at that hour.

Mother saw in the dim light someone approaching the staircase and climbing. The person entered her room. Ma realised who it was and said, "You are the Brahmin cook who lives nearby, am I right?"

"Yes, Ma. I am sorry to come at this late hour. What could I do? I have to work at many places, before I come here . . .."

"It's all right . . .."

Touch Me, That's Enough

"Mother, I want to do pranams, touch your blessed feet...."

Mother laughed, "I don't think anyone should do such a thing to me. After all, I am an ordinary woman, doing whatever job God assigns to me. But since you are keen, I suppose you could do pranams."

"But, I have a problems, Ma. I cannot touch your feet...."

"Why not...?" Mother's voice trailed off.

Great hesitation (a tinge of repugnance) marked the woman. "Mother, I have touched, accidentally, a dog. And unless I bathe, I cannot touch your holy feet."

Mother was flustered. What an orthodox view! What really matters is purity not ritual cleanliness. Why can't people understand that? What a fetish we make of ritual purity! So that the spiritual is merely a ritual. She also remembered her Lord's negation of even the apex of purity: he forbade her from taking those days off in which women are ritually polluted. "It is merely a biological process!" he declared.

"Bath, at this hour?" Mother asked, breaking into speech. "Don't you realise it's past nine? The night, too, is dark."

The Brahmin cook was agitated, "No, Ma, I *have to* take a bath. Otherwise, how can I do pranams to you?"

Mother, perhaps, was amused. By the paradox. The woman certainly believes in her as a living Goddess, a Devi. Yet, she does not heed her advice. They have their own notions to live by. Is Mahamaya so powerful to throw them into such confusion? "Here I am whom this lady regards as the Divine Mother and yet she does not accept my advice!" She decided to try again. "Do one thing. Just go wash your hands and feet and change your clothes. That's more than enough."

Orthodoxy is no such tender shoot on slushy soil to be plucked easily. "That won't do Mother! I have got to have a bath."

Mother tried another specific: "My child! Why don't you listen to *me*? Okay, since you have rejected that, take some Ganges water and sprinkle it on your body. After all, water of Ganga, Thakur used to say, purifies everything!"

The cook was still stubborn, adamant. Unwilling to accept an alternative. Even when it comes from the Divine Mother Herself. Mother rules out a bath and recommended a wash, instead. But that won't do. She then tried Ganges water. In vain. But Mother knew for certain one thing: for all her orthodoxy, the woman was a staunch devotee. The only thing is to break the hard crust of ritualistic dogmatism. And that was what was needed. Mother didn't hesitate. In ringing tones that concealed nothing, Mother said: "OK! *Come, child, and touch me*! That's enough!"

Touch that transforms everything. Or rather brings out the true nature of everything. And everything in and by its very nature is pure!

But in another context, Ma says, "Touch me from a distance." So don't get away with the feeling that she allows everyone to touch her feet!

Chapter Thirty-Two
Forgive Her, She Doesn't Know What She Is Doing

Strange, indeed, are the lives of Godmen and women. Try to understand and you will be caught in knots. One knot you think you unraveled, instantly another gets knotted. Nothing makes sense. They get into contexts which hardly correlate themselves with their radiant being. Perhaps, they get involved in such incidents only to show and, through the show, instruct us. The experience and the example first, then the message and the precept.

"Radhi, listen! You are a mother now. With a child to look after! Give up your addictions and all other antics. Be a good girl and be a good mother to your child!" said Mother.

Mother was dressing vegetables in the kitchen. Radhu was her niece and recently had a child. She was herself sickly, mentally impaired. Mother looked after her with a rare dedication. Something that was her very nature. She bore, cheerfully, the incredibly intolerant tensions it involved.

Mother never could have enough even to eat a nourishing meal. And Master forbade her from stretching her hand before anyone. Her health broke down and she was having bouts of fever.

One cannot contemplate this phase of her life without breaking down in tears. It was sorrow, the sorrow of the Primordial Mother, the Eternal Feminine, for her children. Prodigal children, most.

Radhi was ready with her petulance: "Auntie! I know all that. But I want money for, you know, my dose of opium. I *have* to have it. No matter what."

Mother, one could imagine, felt a weariness strange in her. It was time, she thought, that she made things plain. She was in the middle of finishing the kitchen chores. With a voice that reflected her mood, she said, "Radhi, it is time you got out of all this. You must look after yourself now. I can no longer take care of you. Even my devotion is affected. I came very near to losing everything. I just cannot give you any more money."

Every word hit Radhu vehemently. She never imagined that her gentle aunt could be so forthright. Unable to control her anger, she quickly grasped an eggplant and threw it at Mother with full force. It landed with a thud on Mother's back and she cried and curved her back in pain!

Oh my God! One feels like shouting. The Divine Mother hit with a vegetable and the pain registering on her *Bhagavata deha*! Isn't it strange, for the devotee inexplicable, intolerable? But then what Ma did instantly is what makes her the Mother of all of us! By this time a swelling appeared. She knew the sacrilege of the act.

Unconcerned with the pain, Mother rushed to the photograph of

Forgive Her, She Doesn't Know What She Is Doing

the Master and implored: "Lord! I know Radhu behaved in an unpardonable way. Inexcusable. But you know very well, she is imbalanced, retarded. What do we do with such a kid? Except forgive! For, she doesn't know what she is doing. You are an ocean of compassion. Do forgive her!"

Then Ma did something more. She took a little of the dust of her feet and put it on Radhu's head. Strange, isn't it? Not so, when we recall what the Master said: "If I get angry, you may not receive any punishment. But if she gets angry none, not even I, can save you from that." The dust of her feet is obviously protective, preventing any calamity overtaking that hapless child.

By this time, Radhi, presumably, sobered a bit. Mother drew near and with compassion enveloping everything there, told Radhi: "You know, my Lord and Master never used a harsh word to me! He didn't even call me *tui* but always the respectful *tumi*. And *you* occasion so much pain to this body. So much distress."

And in one of those rare moments of revelation, beloved Mother said: "Do you have any idea, even the remotest, of who I am and where my place is? Simply because I live with you all, without any apparent divine insignia, you think nothing of me!"

That is Ma's mystery, the impenetrable mask of the ordinary, always concealing, fond of anonymity: the gentle dew that drops unseen and unheard! No wonder Radhi instinctively burst into tears. As we all do now, smiling tears of surpassing joy!

Chapter Thirty-Three
Nothing Is Valueless: Everything Is Vibrant

In the cosmos, nothing created by the Creator is valueless. Even the things which appear trash and therefore disposable can be put to use. You need not even recycle the thing used and about to be thrown away. In its very form as it exists, one can put it to use. In nature, nothing is without a function but that it can be put to multiple uses does not strike us. That is because of inner indifference.

By temperament Ma, we notice, is careful in the use of things. Just as she made maximum use of the incredibly small space in the *nahabat*, and never felt cramped, she made multiple uses of everything. A quality she must have had not only innately but also observed in her Lord and Master.

For the incident we are going to contemplate, a wonderful scene took place earlier as a sort of preamble. Golap Ma requested the Holy Mother—who was drying her hair on the roof—to come down and offer the food in the shrine room to Thakur and the image of Gopala. Accordingly, Mother did. "Like a bashful young bride," we are told she said to Sri Ramakrishna "in a soft voice, 'come now; your meal is ready.' Then she came to the image of Gopala and said, 'O my Gopala, come for your meal.'" She told Sarayubala who was seeing all this: "I am inviting them all to their midday meal." And Sarayubala reports that Mother's "earnestness and devotion made me feel that the Deities, as it were, listened to her words and followed her to the offering room." "I was," she declares, "pinned to the ground with wonder."

Wonder because we are not used to the fact Ma perceives: nothing in this vibrant nature is *mrinmaya*, everything is *chinmaya*. The apparently most trivial is or can be put to function in many contexts. After taking her meal, Mother was resting. Then came a devotee with a basket of fruits. He told the monks there in the lower part of the building: "Swamis! Here are some fruits for offering to the Lord!"

"Very Good. We will offer it during the *puja*." They took out the fruits and kept them separately in a plate. They gave the empty basket back to the devotee.

"What shall I do with the basket?" he asked.

"What does one do with an empty basket? Throw it out on one side of the road," said one of the monks.

Mother was, by this time, on the porch. From there she could see the lane and noticed the basket lying on one side of the road. Sarayu was watching Ma's reaction. There was a slight frown on her placid, tranquil face. "See dear! Such a dainty piece! And they throw it away nonchalantly. Perhaps, the monks think this is detachment! But then detachment does not mean we shouldn't put a thing to many uses. Why should we waste anything?

"Yes, Ma . . .. We could certainly use it. It is a brand new one," Sarayu said.

"That's my point. Don't you think, we could use it for at least keeping the peelings of vegetables?" Ma asked.

"Yes. That is a perfect use for something thrown away as useless," Sarayubala agreed.

Ma asked someone to go and fetch the basket. When it was brought back, Mother's delight was visible. "See how skilful these people are to make such an elegantly useful thing!" she said.

One recalls a similar incident. Someone swept the room and threw the broom away, carelessly, into a corner. Ma saw this. She was evidently upset and said: "So your work is over and you throw it away, and don't bother to keep it in its place with care. My child, the time taken to throw is aside and keep it carefully is almost the same. Remember, even the broom is a member of this family and treat it with affection."

What an elevating message from a commonplace incident.